AAT

AQ2016

ADVANCED DIPLOMA IN ACCOUNTING

Synoptic Assessment

EXAM KIT

This Exam Kit supports study for the following AAT qualifications:
AAT Advanced Diploma in Accounting – Level 3
AAT Advanced Certificate in Bookkeeping – Level 3
AAT Advanced Diploma in Accounting at SCQF – Level 6

Kaplan Feedback
Tell us what you think

PUBLISHING

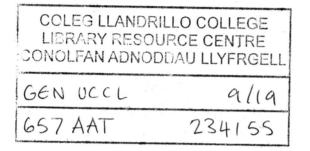
British Library Cataloguing-in-Publication Data

A catalogue record for this book is available from the British Library.

Published by:

Kaplan Publishing UK

Unit 2 The Business Centre

Molly Millar's Lane

Wokingham

Berkshire

RG41 2QZ

ISBN: 978-1-78740-009-2

CONTENTS

Features in this exam kit

In addition to providing a wide ranging bank of real exam style questions, we have also included in this kit:

- unit-specific information and advice on exam technique

- our recommended approach to make your revision for this particular unit as effective as possible.

You will find a wealth of other resources to help you with your studies on the AAT website:

www.aat.org.uk/

Quality and accuracy are of the utmost importance to us so if you spot an error in any of our products, please send an email to mykaplanreporting@kaplan.com with full details, or follow the link to the feedback form in MyKaplan.

Our Quality Co-ordinator will work with our technical team to verify the error and take action to ensure it is corrected in future editions.

SYNOPTIC ASSESSMENT

AAT AQ16 introduces a Synoptic Assessment, which students must complete if they are to achieve the appropriate qualification upon completion of a qualification. In the case of the Advanced Diploma in Accounting, students must pass all of the mandatory assessments and the Synoptic Assessment to achieve the qualification.

As a Synoptic Assessment is attempted following completion of individual units, it draws upon knowledge and understanding from those units. It may be appropriate for students to retain their study materials for individual units until they have successfully completed the Synoptic Assessment for that qualification.

All units within the Advanced Diploma in Accounting are mandatory. Four units are assessed individually in end of unit assessments, but this qualification also includes a synoptic assessment, sat towards the end of the qualification, which draws on and assesses knowledge and understanding from across the qualification:

- Advanced Bookkeeping – end of unit assessment

- Final Accounts Preparation – end of unit assessment

- Management Accounting: Costing – end of unit assessment

- Indirect Tax – end of unit assessment

- Ethics for accountants – assessed within the synoptic assessment only

- Spreadsheets for Accounting – assessed within the synoptic assessment only

Summary of learning outcomes from underlying units which are assessed in the synoptic assessment

Underlying unit	Learning outcomes required
Advanced Bookkeeping	LO1, LO2, LO3, LO4, LO5
Final Accounts Preparation	LO1, LO2, LO3, LO4, LO5, LO6
Management Accounting: Costing	LO1, LO2, LO3, LO4, LO5
Indirect Tax	LO1, LO2, LO3, LO4
Ethics for Accountants	LO1, LO2, LO3, LO4, LO5
Spreadsheets for Accounting	LO1, LO2, LO3, LO4, LO5

FORMAT OF THE ASSESSMENT

The specimen synoptic assessment comprises seven tasks and covers all seven assessment objectives. Students will be assessed by computer-based assessment. Marking of the assessment is partially by computer and partially human marked.

In any one assessment, students may not be assessed on all content, or on the full depth or breadth of a piece of content. The content assessed may change over time to ensure validity of assessment, but all assessment criteria will be tested over time.

The following weighting is based upon the AAT Qualification Specification documentation which may be subject to variation.

	Assessment objective	Weighting
AO1	Demonstrate an understanding of the relevance of the ethical code for accountants, the need to act ethically in a given situation, and the appropriate action to take in reporting questionable behaviour	15%
AO2	Prepare accounting and VAT records and respond to errors, omissions and other concerns, in accordance with accounting and ethical principles and relevant regulations	16%
AO3	Demonstrate an understanding of the inter-relationship between the financial accounting and management accounting systems of an organisation and how they can be used to support managers in decision making	14%
AO4	Apply ethical and accounting principles when preparing final accounts for different types of organisation, develop ethical courses of action and communicate relevant information effectively	15%
AO5	Demonstrate a range of spreadsheet knowledge and skills when working with accounting data	10%
AO6	Use relevant spreadsheet skills to analyse, interpret and report management accounting data Prepare financial accounting information, comprising extended trial balances and final accounts for sole traders and partnerships, using spreadsheets	16%
AO7	Prepare financial accounting information, comprising extended trial balances and final accounts for sole traders and partnerships, using spreadsheets	14%
	Total	100%

Time allowed: 3 hours and 15 minutes

PASS MARK: The pass mark for all AAT assessments is 70%.

🕐 **Always keep your eye on the clock and make sure you attempt all questions!**

The detailed syllabus and study guide written by the AAT can be found at:

www.aat.org.uk/

ASSESSMENT OBJECTIVES

To perform this synoptic assessment effectively you need to know and understand the following:

Assessment objective 1	Demonstrate an understanding of the relevance of the ethical code for accountants, the need to act ethically in a given situation, and the appropriate action to take in reporting questionable behaviour
Related learning objectives	**Ethics for Accountants** LO1 Understand the need to act ethically LO2 Understand the relevance to the accountant's work of the ethical code for professional accountants LO4 Identify action to take in relation to unethical behaviour or illegal acts
Assessment objective 2	Prepare accounting and VAT records and respond to errors, omissions and other concerns, in accordance with accounting and ethical principles and relevant regulations
Related learning objectives	**Indirect Tax** LO1 Understand and apply VAT legislation requirements LO2 Accurately complete VAT returns and submit them in a timely manner LO3 Understand implications of errors, omissions and late filing and payment LO4 Report VAT related information in accordance with regulatory and organisational requirement **Ethics for Accountants** LO3 Recognise how to act ethically in an accounting role LO4 Identify action to take in relation to unethical behaviour or illegal acts **Advanced Bookkeeping** LO1 Apply the principles of advanced double-entry bookkeeping LO2 Implement procedures for the acquisition and disposal of non-current assets LO3 Prepare and record depreciation calculations LO4 Record period end adjustments **Final Accounts Preparation** LO2 Explain the need for final accounts and the accounting and ethical principles underlying their preparation LO3 Prepare accounting records from incomplete information

Assessment objective 3	Demonstrate an understanding of the inter-relationship between the financial accounting and management accounting systems of an organisation and how they can be used to support managers in decision making
Related learning objectives	**Advanced Bookkeeping** LO3 Prepare and record depreciation calculations LO4 Record period end adjustments LO5 Produce and extend the trial balance **Final Accounts Preparation** LO2 Explain the need for final accounts and the accounting and ethical principles underlying their preparation LO3 Prepare accounting records from incomplete information LO4 Produce accounts for sole traders LO5 Produce accounts for partnerships **Management Accounting: Costing** LO1 Understand the purpose and use of management accounting within an organisation LO2 Apply techniques required for dealing with costs LO3 Apportion costs according to organisational requirements LO5 Apply management accounting techniques to support decision making
Assessment objective 4	Apply ethical and accounting principles when preparing final accounts for different types of organisation, develop ethical courses of action and communicate relevant information effectively
Related learning objectives	**Ethics for Accountants** LO3 Recognise how to act ethically in an accounting role **Final Accounts Preparation** LO1 Distinguish between the financial recording and reporting requirements of different types of organisation LO2 Explain the need for final accounts and the accounting and ethical principles underlying their preparation LO3 Prepare accounting records from incomplete information LO4 Produce accounts for sole traders LO5 Produce accounts for partnerships LO6 Recognise the key differences between preparing accounts for a limited company and a sole trader

Assessment objective 5	Demonstrate a range of spreadsheet knowledge and skills when working with accounting data
Related learning objectives	**Spreadsheets for Accounting** LO1 Design and structure appropriate spreadsheets to meet customer needs LO2 Use spreadsheet software to record, format and organise data LO3 Use relevant tools to manipulate and analyse data LO4 Use software tools to verify accuracy and protect data LO5 Use tools and techniques to prepare and report accounting information
Assessment objective 6	Use relevant spreadsheet skills to analyse, interpret and report management accounting data
Related learning objectives	**Management Accounting: Costing** LO1 Understand the purpose and use of management accounting within an organisation LO3 Apportion costs according to organisational requirements LO4 Analyse and review deviations from budget and report these to management LO5 Apply management accounting techniques to support decision making **Spreadsheets for Accounting** LO1 Design and structure appropriate spreadsheets to meet customer needs LO2 Use spreadsheet software to record, format and organise data LO3 Use relevant tools to manipulate and analyse data LO5 Use tools and techniques to prepare and report accounting information
Assessment objective 7	Prepare financial accounting information, comprising extended trial balances and final accounts for sole traders and partnerships, using spreadsheets
Related learning objectives	**Final Accounts Preparation** LO4 Produce accounts for sole traders LO5 Produce accounts for partnerships **Advanced Bookkeeping** LO5 Produce and extend the trial balance **Spreadsheets for Accounting** LO1 Design and structure appropriate spreadsheets to meet customer needs LO2 Use spreadsheet software to record, format and organise data LO3 Use relevant tools to manipulate and analyse data LO4 Use software tools to verify accuracy and protect data LO5 Use tools and techniques to prepare and report accounting information

INDEX TO QUESTIONS AND ANSWERS

KAPLAN PUBLISHING

NOTE: The answers to the tasks in these scenarios can be found as spreadsheet files on your MyKaplan account (together with the text and word files required).

EXAM TECHNIQUE

- **Do not skip any of the material** in the syllabus.

- **Read each question** *very* carefully.

- **Double-check your answer** before committing yourself to it.

- Answer **every** question – if you do not know an answer to a multiple choice question or true/false question, you don't lose anything by guessing. Think carefully before you **guess**.

- If you are answering a multiple-choice question, **eliminate first those answers that you know are wrong.** Then choose the most appropriate answer from those that are left.

- **Don't panic** if you realise you've answered a question incorrectly. Getting one question wrong will not mean the difference between passing and failing.

Computer-based exams – tips

- Do not attempt a CBA until you have **completed all study material** relating to it.

- On the AAT website there is a CBA demonstration. It is **ESSENTIAL** that you attempt this before your real CBA. You will become familiar with how to move around the CBA screens and the way that questions are formatted, increasing your confidence and speed in the actual exam.

- Be sure you understand how to use the **software** before you start the exam. If in doubt, ask the assessment centre staff to explain it to you.

- Questions are **displayed on the screen** and answers are entered using keyboard and mouse. At the end of the exam, in the case of those units not subject to human marking, you are given a certificate showing the result you have achieved.

- In addition to the traditional multiple-choice question type, CBAs will also contain **other types of questions**, such as number entry questions, drag and drop, true/false, pick lists or drop down menus or hybrids of these.

- In some CBAs you will have to type in complete computations or written answers.

- You need to be sure you **know how to answer questions** of this type before you sit the exam, through practice.

KAPLAN PUBLISHING

KAPLAN'S RECOMMENDED REVISION APPROACH

QUESTION PRACTICE IS THE KEY TO SUCCESS

Success in professional examinations relies upon you acquiring a firm grasp of the required knowledge at the tuition phase. In order to be able to do the questions, knowledge is essential.

However, the difference between success and failure often hinges on your exam technique on the day and making the most of the revision phase of your studies.

The **Kaplan Study Text** is the starting point, designed to provide the underpinning knowledge to tackle all questions. However, in the revision phase, poring over text books is not the answer.

Kaplan Pocket Notes are designed to help you quickly revise a topic area; however you then need to practise questions. There is a need to progress to exam style questions as soon as possible, and to tie your exam technique and technical knowledge together.

The importance of question practice cannot be over-emphasised.

The recommended approach below is designed by expert tutors in the field, in conjunction with their knowledge of the examiner and the specimen assessment.

You need to practise as many questions as possible in the time you have left.

OUR AIM

Our aim is to get you to the stage where you can attempt exam questions confidently, to time, in a closed book environment, with no supplementary help (i.e. to simulate the real examination experience).

Practising your exam technique is also vitally important for you to assess your progress and identify areas of weakness that may need more attention in the final run up to the examination.

In order to achieve this we recognise that initially you may feel the need to practice some questions with open book help.

Good exam technique is vital.

THE KAPLAN REVISION PLAN

Stage 1: Assess areas of strengths and weaknesses

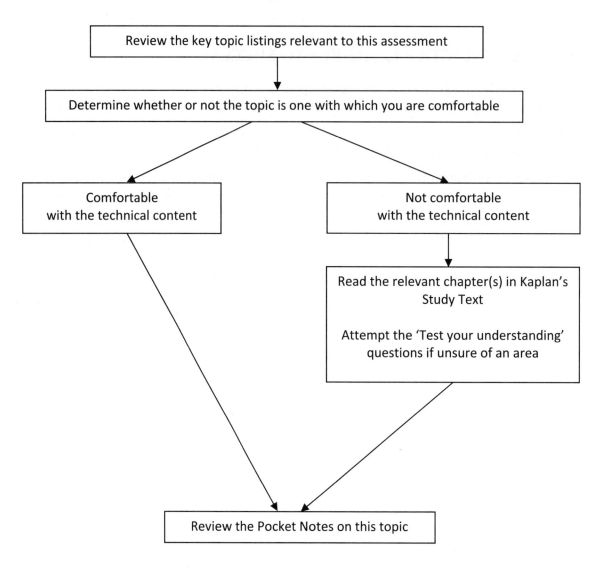

Stage 2: Practice questions

Follow the order of revision of topics as presented in this Kit and attempt the questions in the order suggested.

Try to avoid referring to Study Texts and your notes and the model answer until you have completed your attempt.

Review your attempt with the model answer and assess how much of the answer you achieved.

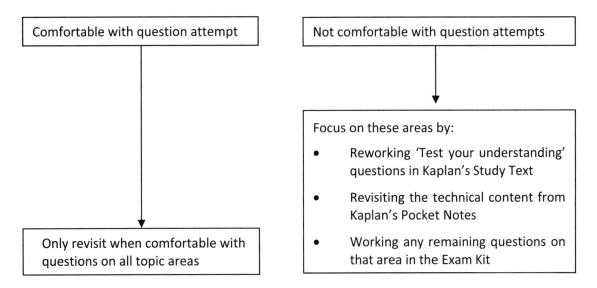

Comfortable with question attempt

Not comfortable with question attempts

Focus on these areas by:

- Reworking 'Test your understanding' questions in Kaplan's Study Text
- Revisiting the technical content from Kaplan's Pocket Notes
- Working any remaining questions on that area in the Exam Kit

Only revisit when comfortable with questions on all topic areas

Stage 3: Final pre-exam revision

We recommend that you **attempt at least one mock examination** containing a set of previously unseen exam-standard questions.

Attempt the mock CBA online in timed, closed book conditions to simulate the real exam experience.

Section 1

EXAM – PART I – PRACTICE TASKS

TASK 1.1

Assessment objective 1	Demonstrate an understanding of the relevance of the ethical code for accountants, the need to act ethically in a given situation, and the appropriate action to take in reporting questionable behaviour

1   DILIGENCE

Conner, a member in practice, has just received a call from a potential new client asking him to help in a business transaction. However when asked for her address, the client said she would rather not say.

Advise Conner on how to respond to the client.

	Yes	No
Continue with forging a relationship with the client in the usual manner		
Inform the client that without knowing the correct address the client/accountant relationship cannot be forged		
Consider reporting the conversation to NCA.		

2   JESS

Jessica, a member in practice, has been tasked to complete an important assignment. However, she knows that she will not have enough time complete the work properly.

Indicate which fundamental ethical principle is under threat. Select ONE answer only.

Integrity	
Confidentiality	
Professional competence and due care	
Professional behaviour	
Objectivity	

3 REFERENCE

Steve is a professional accountant working in practice.

Kept Ltd is Steve's oldest client and as well as the usual accountancy and tax services, Steve has recently been asked to write a reference to a new landlord confirming that Kept Ltd is likely to be able to pay its rent for the next 3 years.

While this would normally not be a problem, Steve is aware that Kept Ltd has been experiencing financial difficulties over the last 6 months, so he is wary of writing such a reference. To reassure him, the Chief accountant has offered to pay Steve a large fee for supplying the reference and suggested Steve should include a disclaimer of liability.

Required:

(a)   **Analyse Steve's dilemma from an ethical point of view.**

(b)   **If Steve writes the reference, knowing Kept Ltd may not be able to pay, what crime is he potentially committing?**

(c)   **What difference would it make if Steve included a disclaimer of liability in the written reference?**

4 CYCLE

Mthbe is a professional accountant with his own small practice. He performs accountancy and tax services for a wide range of small clients including many sole traders.

Required:

(a)   **Explain, with justification, TWO areas in which Mthbe needs to keep his technical knowledge up-to-date.**

(b)   **According to the AAT CPD policy how often should Mthbe complete a CPD Cycle?**

(c)   **List the recommended stages in the AAT's CPD cycle.**

5 SARAH

Sarah is an AAT member working for a small accountancy practice.

She has received a call from a property agent asking for the following information about a client.

*   Accounts for the previous three years.

*   An assurance that they will be able to meet the rent for a proposed property rental.

Required:

(a)   **Advise Sarah on the appropriate course of action, with regards to giving the agent the Accounts for the previous three years.**

(b)   **Advise Sarah on the appropriate course of action, with regards to giving the agent an assurance the client will be able to pay.**

6 KUTCHINS

Gemma is an AAT member working for Kutchins Ltd, an engineering consultancy. She has recently started this job, having previously worked for an accountancy firm where she was the audit senior for Kirk Ltd, a competitor of Kutchins Ltd.

Required:

Explain whether Gemma is allowed to use knowledge, information and experience gained from her previous employer in her new job.

7 BEVIS

Bevis, an AAT member, has just joined a building company as a management accountant, after working for some years in a local accountancy practice.

The following situations have arisen in Bevis' first week at work.

Matter 1

When he first joined the company the Managing Director invited him out to lunch so that they could get to know each other. The Managing Director spent most of the time questioning Bevis about competitors who were clients of the firm Bevis used to work for.

Matter 2

As part of Bevis' work he needed to find out some information on behalf of the customer. When Bevis made the necessary phone call Bevis was told that the organisation did not have authority from the customer to disclose the information. When Bevis told his boss he told Bevis to ring back and pretend to be the customer.

Required:

Explain what Bevis should do in respect of the two matters above.

8 NIGHT OUT

Bella, a professional accountant, was invited on a 'night out' with others from the accounts department. This became quite a boisterous evening and it ended with the Finance Director removing a sign from the front of a shop which he brought into the office the next day as a reminder of the good evening.

Required:

(a) **Indicate which fundamental ethical principle is under threat. Select ONE answer only.**

Integrity	
Confidentiality	
Professional competence and due care	
Professional behaviour	
Objectivity	

(b) **Indicate what course of action Bella should take.**

Do nothing – a sign is not worth losing your job over	
Suggest to the FD that he should replace the sign	

9   DILEMMA

Your boss has told you that there are going to be some redundancies in the company. You will not be affected, but he has named a number of people who will be, including a good friend of yours who is in the process of buying a holiday home in Cornwall. You know that your friend would not be able to afford the property if she were to lose her job and that she would pull out of the purchase if she knew about the redundancy plans.

The news of the redundancies will not be made public for several weeks.

Required:

(a)   Indicate which fundamental ethical principle is under threat. Select ONE answer only.

Integrity	
Confidentiality	
Professional competence and due care	
Professional behaviour	
Objectivity	

(b)   Indicate your best course of action

From an ethical point of view you should tell your friend about the redundancies on the grounds it could save her unnecessary financial problems and distress.	
You should not tell your friend about the redundancies.	

10   JUSTIN

Justin is an AAT member in practice at Tipling LLP. He is a senior on an assurance assignment for Brittle plc. He inherits a 10% shareholding in this client.

Required:

(a)   Which type of threat does this situation represent?

Self-interest threat	
Self-review threat	
Intimidation threat	
Advocacy threat	
Familiarity threat	

(b)   What would Justin's best course of action be?

Continue as senior but make the partners aware of the inheritance	
Ask to be removed from the assignment	
Resign from Tipling LLP	
Report the matter to the National Crime Agency (NCA)	

11   JULIE

Julie has audited the accounts of Believe It plc as part of the assurance team for the past five years. She has been approached by Believe It plc with an offer of the Senior Accountant role.

Required:

(a)   **State which type of threat this situation represent.**

(b)   **Suggest TWO safeguards the assurance firm should have in place concerning such a threat.**

12   NO DEFENCE

M plc is a large UK-based building firm that specialises in public sector contracts such as schools, hospitals and sports facilities.

Having a strong green and ethical reputation is vital to M plc's chances of winning government contracts. To protect its reputation, M has an internal ethics hotline for employees to raise any concerns they might have or evidence of wrongdoing.

Ever since the economic downturn in 2008, M plc has seen a major decline in its European business so the Board are keen to expand in other parts of the world.

Matter

In 2013 M plc was successful in winning a major contract to build new hospitals in Country H in Africa. However, a month later, the ethics hotline received a call concerning Mr Igbinadola, the agent who represented M plc in the negotiations with the government. The call claimed that Mr Igbinadola is well known for his excessive gifts and hospitality and paid for the MP involved in the negotiations to go on a lavish holiday just weeks before the contract was awarded. The Board of M plc claims no knowledge of such gifts and is adamant it didn't authorise this.

Required:

(a)   **Outline the four offences described by the UK Bribery Act 2010.**

(b)   **Explain the defences a commercial organisation could offer to a charge of bribery.**

(c)   **Discuss whether M plc could be guilty of an offence under the UK Bribery Act 2010.**

13   L PLC

Andre, an AAT member, works for L plc, a UK company that exports a range of seed and other agricultural products to growers around the globe.

Recently Andre accompanied other representatives from L to go to a foreign country ('M') to discuss with a local farming cooperative the possible supply of a new strain of wheat that is resistant to a disease which recently swept the region.

In the meeting, the head of the cooperative told them about the problems which the relative unavailability of antiretroviral drugs cause locally in the face of a high HIV infection rate.

In a subsequent meeting with an official of M to discuss the approval of L's new wheat strain for import, the official suggests that L could pay for the necessary antiretroviral drugs and that this will be a very positive factor in the Government's consideration of the licence to import the new seed strain.

In a further meeting, the same official states that L should donate money to a certain charity suggested by the official which, the official assures, will then take the necessary steps to purchase and distribute the drugs.

Andre has raised concerns regarding potential bribery risks if L goes ahead with the suggestions made. However, the government official concerned has assured Andre that such payments comply with local laws and are standard custom and practice.

Required:

Advise the Directors of L plc, from the perspective of bribery risk.

14   IN-HOUSE CODE

The directors of John Groom Ltd, a small manufacturing company, have drafted an ethical code for use within the organisation, based on ones used by competitors and the industry trade organisation. The Board also plan to encourage suppliers to adopt the code.

Required:

Explain the legal status of this code.

15   NEW CODE

Matter

Cosby plc owns a small chain of supermarkets with an emphasis on organic, local produce. The Directors of Cosby plc are concerned that, despite having better quality produce than rivals, it is not competing as well as it would like against national supermarket chains.

The Marketing Director has proposed that Cosby plc should set up a new corporate code of ethics that could be used as part of its marketing effort. He is convinced that many customers will be influenced by such a code and has suggested that the following aspects could be incorporated:

1   All products should be purchased from local farms and suppliers where appropriate.

2   All packing materials should be obtained from renewable sources where feasible.

3   All suppliers to be paid on time.

4   All suppliers to be paid fair prices as determined by the Purchasing Manager.

Required:

Comment on EACH of the ethical values suggested by the Marketing Director, highlighting the benefit of each, together with any reservations you may have concerning them.

16 PROCEDURE

Ye Lin, an AAT member, works for a C plc, a company that is now under investigation for corruption. The Finance Director has told Ye Lin not to cooperate with the investigation team.

Required:

(a) State whether Ye Lin should cooperate with the investigation or obey the FD.

| She should cooperate with the investigation | |
| She should refuse to cooperate as it would breach confidentiality | |

(b) State what Ye Lin could be found guilty of if she fails to cooperate with the investigation.

Misconduct	
Money laundering	
Whistleblowing	

(c) Indicate which of the following disciplinary actions the AAT could apply if Ye Lin is found guilty of damaging the reputation of the association. (Select all that apply)

Lose her job with C plc	
Be expelled from the Association	
Have her membership of the Association suspended	
Have her practicing licence withdrawn.	
Receive a prison sentence	
Have to re-sit all her professional exams	

17 CHRIS

Chris, an AAT member, works for HJK and Co, a medium sized accountancy practice based in Manchester. Chris has performed accountancy and tax services for both Yin Ltd and Yang Ltd for many years.

Yin Ltd is currently in negotiations with the Board of Yang Ltd concerning a proposed takeover. Both Yin Ltd and Yang Ltd have requested that Chris help advise them.

Required:

(a) State which TWO fundamental principles are threatened by the proposed takeover.

(b) Describe the ethical conflict resolution process Chris should undertake in deciding how to act in respect of this matter. Assume that he will be able to resolve the conflict of interest without needing to seek external professional advice.

(c) Assuming he decides he can act for one of the clients, explain TWO issues Chris must consider when carrying out his work.

18   SIMON

Simon, a member in practise, inherits from his Grandfather shares in a company that his firm audits.

Required:

(a)   **State which threat this situation represents.**

(b)   **Outline what Simon's best course of action is.**

19   LAST

Jason is an AAT member in practice. The following matter arose this week:

Matter

One evening Jason had a drink with an old friend, Brian, an AAT member currently working as an accountant for a large manufacturing company.

Brian was extremely worried about events in the company he works for. He had been asked by one of the directors to become involved in an arrangement that would lead to personal financial gain for the director at the expense of the company. Brian had been offered financial reward for this, and it had been made clear to him that he would lose his job if he didn't comply.

Required:

(a)   **State which ethical principle Brian has already breached by talking about this situation?**

(b)   **Explain what course of action is most appropriate for Brian to take immediately.**

(c)   **If the situation cannot be resolved via internal action, explain what Brian should do.**

20   SAFE AND SOUND

Lara is a professional accountant in practice. Detailed below are three matters that have arisen with respect to some of Lara's clients.

Matter A

The director of Company W, a listed company, sold a substantial shareholding prior to the announcement of worse than expected results for the company.

Matter B

Mike is CEO of Company X and is also a non-executive director of Company Y and sits on the remuneration committee of that company.

Graham is CEO of Company Y and is also a non-executive director of Company X and sits on the remuneration committee of that company.

Mike and Graham are good friends and play golf together every Saturday.

Matter C

The chairman of Company Z does not like conflict on the board.

When a new director is appointed, the chairman always ensures that the director's family members obtain highly paid jobs in the company and, in the case of children, that they are sponsored by Company Z through college.

Company Z is very profitable, although the board appears to be ineffective in querying the actions of the chairman.

Required:

For each of the situations above, identify the ethical threat to the client and recommend an ethical safeguard, explaining why that safeguard is appropriate.

21 FREE HOLIDAYS

Sarah works for a firm of accountants called B & Sons LLP and has recently introduced a new client to the firm called Leigh Davis. She has also been appointed as the audit manager for the client's company A Tours Limited which specialises in luxury holidays in the Caribbean. Leigh Davis was keen for Sarah to be appointed the audit manager for his company as he has known Sarah for a long time. He has recently offered Sarah free holidays in the Caribbean in return for her not asking questions about some irregularities in his company's financial statements.

Required:

Analyse the above scenario from the perspective of the law relating bribery. In particular, explain which criminal offences the various parties have committed or are at risk of committing.

22 KEN

Ken is involved in illegal activities, from which he makes a considerable amount of money.

In order to conceal his gains from the illegal activities, he bought a bookshop intending to pass off his illegally gained money as profits from the legitimate bookshop business.

Ken employs Los to act as the manager of the bookshop and Mel as his accountant to produce false business accounts for the bookshop business.

Required:

(a) **Explain what is meant by money laundering, the different categories of offence and possible punishments.**

(b) **Analyse the above scenario from the perspective of the law relating to money laundering. In particular, explain which criminal offences may have been committed by the various parties.**

23   MLRO

Jeff, a member in practice has recently come across what he believes is an investigation by the regulatory authorities into allegations of money laundering at a large client.

Required:

(a)   **Jeff decides to communicate this to the Finance Director of the client. What offence Jeff will commit if he does this?**

Breach of confidentiality	
Tipping off	
Money laundering	

(b)   **What is the maximum sentence that Jeff can receive if found guilty of the offence.**

	Years

(c)   **Jeff's defence includes the claim that his organisation does not have a MLRO (Money Laundering Reporting Officer). In the absence of an MLRO, who should Jeff have approached with his concerns?**

HMRC	
The National Crime Agency (NCA)	
The national press	

(d)   **A second part of Jeff's defence is that the amount in question was only £3,000 and that this is below the *de minimis* limit. What is the *de minimis* limit?**

£	

24   ADAM

Adam, an AAT member within the UK, works for a firm of accountants, LOFT and Co, with a range of clients.

Matter 1

Adam has found an error in a client's tax affairs. The client has refused to disclose this known error, even after Adam has given notice of this error and an appropriate amount of time has been allowed to take action.

Required:

State to whom Adam is obliged to report this refusal to and the information surrounding it.

Matter 2

LOFT and Co recently billed a client, H Ltd, £5,000 and were very surprised when they received a cheque for £50,000 in settlement of the invoice.

The Finance Director of H Ltd explained that it was a mistake on his part but asked whether LOFT and Co could send a cheque for the overpayment of £45,000 to Q Ltd, a different company and not one of LOFT's clients.

Required:

Discuss whether or not LOFT and Co should agree to the payment.

25   DONNA

Donna, an accountant in practice, has recently been working on the tax computations for a client, Stoppard plc.

In preparing this year's tax returns Donna realised that she made an error preparing the last tax returns which resulted in an underpayment. She told the Finance Director of Stoppard plc about the error but he is refusing to tell the HMRC, claiming 'she made the mistake, not him'.

Indicate whether the following statements are true or false.

	True	False
Funds retained after discovery of a tax error amount to money laundering by Stoppard plc		
Donna should report the matter to the National Crime Agency (NCA)		
Donna needs to make an authorised disclosure to the National Crime Agency NCA		

TASK 1.2

Assessment objective 2	Prepare accounting and VAT records and respond to errors, omissions and other concerns, in accordance with accounting and ethical principles and relevant regulations

26   EMMA

Emma is a sole trader and is registered for value added tax (VAT). In the quarter ended 31 March 2017 Emma had the following transactions:

Sales (exclusive of VAT where applicable)

Standard rated	£450,000
Zero rated	£20,000

Purchases and expenses

Purchases of inventory (all standard rated and exclusive of VAT)	£180,000

Expenses (inclusive of VAT where applicable)

Wages	£120,000
Electricity	£40,000
Motoring expenses (all business)	£15,000

A discount of 4% on all sales is offered to customers if invoices are paid within 30 days. Invoices, representing £225,000 of standard rated sales and £10,000 of zero rated sales, were paid within this time during the quarter ended 31 March 2017. These figures are exclusive of VAT.

Debts of £1,200 and £900 (exclusive of VAT at 20%), which were due on 1 February 2016 and 13 October 2016 respectively, were written off by Emma in March 2017.

Required:

Calculate the value added tax (VAT) payable or reclaimable by Emma for the quarter ended 31 March 2017.

27   MONTY FINCH

(a)   Monty Finch has been trading for the last three years. His annual standard rated sales have recently exceeded the VAT threshold of £83,000 but he has failed to notify HM Revenue and Customs.

Required:

Explain the amount(s) of late notification penalty that could be applied.

(b)   Broad Ltd is registered for VAT.

Required:

State two types of expenditure on which the input VAT payable by a registered trader is treated as 'blocked' and therefore irrecoverable.

28 BOB HAWKES

(a) Bob Hawkes operates a jewellery business and is registered for VAT.

He received an order for a silver and diamond necklace on 14 May 2016. A deposit of £350 was received with the order. The order was completed and delivered on 16 July 2016. An invoice was raised and dispatched on 20 July 2016 and the final (balancing) payment was received on 31 August 2016.

Bob does not operate the cash accounting scheme.

Required:

State how the tax point for VAT purposes is determined and the date(s) which will apply in this case.

(b) **State how the VAT tax point is determined for goods supplied on a sale or return basis.**

(c) **State how the VAT tax point is determined for continuous supplies of services.**

29 YEE-LING

Yee-ling is a sole trader and has recently registered for value added tax (VAT).

Yee-ling understands that it is important to use the correct deemed date of sale (i.e. the tax point). Recently she sold inventory for £3,000. A £400 payment in advance had been received on 28 May 2016 and the inventory was delivered on 24 June 2016. Yee-ling sent an invoice for the balance due of £2,600 on 2 July 2016 and received this amount from the customer on 1 August 2016.

Yee-ling is not in the cash accounting scheme.

Required:

(a) **State how the tax point (time of supply) is determined for the purposes of VAT.**

(b) **State, giving reasons, the tax point(s) in respect of the above transaction made by Yee-ling.**

(c) **Give two reasons why it is important to determine the right tax point.**

30 MARTHA

Martha started her own business on 1 October 2016 and has a taxable turnover of £13,900 per month.

Required:

(a) **State by when Martha must notify HM Revenue and Customs (HMRC) that she is liable to be registered for value added tax (VAT) and from what date the registration would normally be effective.**

(b) **Explain the circumstances in which Martha will be allowed to recover input VAT incurred on goods purchased and services incurred prior to the date of VAT registration.**

31 SEA, SAND AND SURF LTD

Sea, Sand and Surf Ltd (SSS Ltd) is a UK registered company. SSS Ltd is registered for value added tax (VAT).

During the quarter ended 31 December 2016 SSS Ltd carried out the following transactions.

	£
Sales (exclusive of VAT, where applicable):	
Standard rated	120,000
Zero rated	18,000
Purchases (exclusive of VAT):	
Goods for resale (all standard rated)	58,000
Plant and machinery (standard rated)	20,000
Expenses (inclusive of VAT, where applicable):	
Wages of staff	28,000
Electricity	3,525
Accountancy fees	1,410
Buildings insurance (exempt supply)	940

Irrecoverable debts totalling £1,400 (exclusive of VAT) were written off during the above period. This amount comprised two debts, one for £600 due to have been paid in May 2016, and one for £800 due to have been paid in August 2016.

Required:

Calculate the value added tax (VAT) payable or reclaimable by Sea, Sand and Surf Ltd for the quarter ended 31 December 2016.

32 ATHLETIC LTD

Athletic Ltd is a small UK registered company, which is not yet registered for value added tax (VAT). The company started to trade on 1 December 2016 and its forecast total sales for the periods shown are expected to be:

1 December 2016 to 28 February 2017	£22,000
1 March 2017 to 31 May 2017	£24,000
1 June 2017 to 31 August 2017	£57,000

You should assume that all sales are of taxable items and are made evenly throughout the periods shown. The above figures are exclusive of VAT.

Required:

(a) **State the date by which Athletic Ltd will have to notify HM Revenue and Customs (HMRC) of its need to register for VAT. Include workings to support your answer.**

(b) **State the date from which Athletic Ltd should charge VAT.**

(c) **On the assumption that Athletic Ltd only makes standard rated sales and does not join the annual accounting scheme, state the length of the company's normal VAT return period and when the VAT return must be received by HMRC.**

(d) **State two advantages and two disadvantages of registering for VAT voluntarily (i.e. when annual turnover is below the annual registration threshold).**

33   EMAIL

You are a junior accountant. Today's date is 16 July 2017.

The company financial accountant has asked you to deal with the VAT return for the quarter ended 30 June 2017.

The VAT payable from the VAT return you have just completed is £11,657.42.

Required:

Draft an email to the financial accountant advising him of the amount of VAT that will be paid or received, how it will be paid, the date due and the impact that the VAT payment may have on the company cash flow and financial forecasts.

34   VECTOR LTD

Vector Ltd is registered for VAT, and is in the process of completing its VAT return for the quarter ended 31 March 2017. The following information is available.

(1)   Sales invoices totalling £128,000 and £40,000 were issued in respect of standard rated sales, and zero rated sales respectively.

(2)   On 15 March 2017 Vector Ltd received an advance deposit of £4,500 (VAT inclusive) in respect of a contract that is due to be completed during April 2017. The total value of the contract is £10,000. No sales invoices had been raised in relation to this contract as at 31 March 2017.

(3)   Standard rated expenses are £74,800, including £4,200 for entertaining UK customers.

(4)   On 31 March 2017 Vector Ltd wrote off £12,000 due from a customer as an irrecoverable debt. The debt was in respect of three invoices, each of £4,000, that were due for payment on 15 August, 15 September and 15 October 2016 respectively. Each invoice had VAT of £800 added to make a total payable by the customer of £4,800.

(5)   On 1 January 2017 the company purchased a motor car costing £9,800 for the use of its sales manager for both private and business purposes.

(6)   On 14 January the company spent £16,500 (VAT inclusive) on a new piece of plant.

Unless indicated otherwise all of the above figures are exclusive of VAT.

Required:

Calculate the amount of VAT payable by Vector Ltd for the quarter ended 31 March 2017.

35   DYNAMO LTD

Dynamo Ltd commenced trading as a wholesaler on 1 November 2016.

Its sales have been as follows:

		£			£
2016	November	4,100	**2017**	June	6,600
	December	4,000		July	6,800
2017	January	4,400		August	7,500
	February	5,000		September	10,100
	March	4,900		October	10,200
	April	5,600		November	11,800
	May	6,500		December	11,900

The company's sales are all standard rated, and the above figures are exclusive of VAT.

Required:

Explain by what date Dynamo Ltd will be required to compulsorily register for VAT, and what action the company must then take.

36   BATTERY LTD

(a)   Battery Ltd only sells goods of high value and at present issues sales invoices that show:

(1)   the invoice date and invoice number

(2)   the type of supply

(3)   the quantity and a description of the goods supplied

(4)   Battery Ltd's name and address, and

(5)   the name and address of the customer.

Required:

State the additional information that Battery Ltd will have to show on its sales invoices in order that these are valid for VAT purposes.

(b)   There are two tests for determining compulsory registration for VAT. One is the past turnover test which looks at the taxable turnover of the last 12 months and the other is the future turnover test.

Required:

Explain how the future turnover test is applied.

37 CONFUSED LTD

(a) Confused Ltd will commence trading in 2017. The company operates a small aeroplane, and is considering three alternative types of business.

These are:

(1) training, in which case all sales will be standard rated for VAT,

(2) transport, in which case all sales will be zero rated for VAT, and

(3) an air ambulance service, in which case all sales will be exempt from VAT.

For each alternative, Confused Ltd's sales will be £84,000 per month (exclusive of VAT), and standard rated expenses will be £10,000 per month (inclusive of VAT).

Required:

For each of the three alternative types of business

(i) state whether Confused Ltd will be required or permitted to register for VAT when trading commences, and

(ii) calculate the monthly amount of output VAT due and input VAT recoverable.

(b) Puzzled Ltd has discovered that a number of errors have been made when preparing its VAT returns for the previous four quarters. As a result of the errors, the company will have to make an additional payment of VAT to HM Revenue and Customs.

Required:

Explain how Puzzled Ltd can voluntarily disclose the errors that have been discovered.

38 VAT ERRORS

The following table shows four possible error situations.

	Net error £	Turnover £
1	24,567	2,000,000
2	4,568	85,400
3	35,980	4,567,090
4	51,600	10,000,000

Required:

For each of the situations, explain whether the non-deliberate error can be corrected on the next VAT return or whether separate disclosure is required.

39 ASTUTE LTD

Astute Ltd registered for VAT on 1 July 2016. The company has annual standard rated sales of £350,000. This figure is inclusive of VAT. Because of bookkeeping problems Astute Ltd has been late in submitting its VAT returns to date.

Required:

Advise Astute Ltd of the conditions that it must satisfy before being permitted to use the VAT annual accounting scheme, and the advantages of joining the scheme.

40   BRIGHT LTD

Bright Ltd registered for VAT on 1 January 2017.

The company will have annual standard rated sales of £75,000 all made to the general public. The company will have annual standard rated expenses of £10,000. Both figures are inclusive of VAT at 20%.

The relevant flat rate scheme percentage for the company's trade is 12%.

Required:

Advise Bright Ltd of the conditions that it must satisfy before being permitted to use the VAT flat rate scheme, and the advantages of joining the scheme.

Your answer should be supported by appropriate calculations of the potential annual tax saving. Ignore the 1% reduction of the flat rate percentage in the first year of VAT registration.

41   CLEVER LTD

Clever Ltd registered for VAT on 1 June 2016. The company has annual standard rated sales of £250,000. This figure is inclusive of VAT. The company pays its expenses on a cash basis, but allows customers three months credit when paying for sales. Several of Clever Ltd's customers have recently defaulted on the payment of their debts.

Required:

Advise Clever Ltd of the conditions that it must satisfy before being permitted to use the VAT cash accounting scheme, and the advantages of joining the scheme.

42   CITY MERCHANDISE LTD

City Merchandise Ltd prepares value added tax (VAT) returns on a quarterly basis. It does not operate the cash accounting scheme.

During the company's quarter ended 31 March 2017 the following transactions occurred:

Standard rated sales	£110,000
Zero rated sales	£30,000
Standard rated purchases	£60,000

The above three amounts are stated exclusive of VAT where applicable.

The company offers a 5% discount to customers who pay within 30 days. Discounts on standard rated invoices totalling £55,000 (VAT exclusive) were settled in this VAT quarter within the 30 day discount period.

The company also paid the following expenses during the same VAT quarter:

Electricity	£4,000
Wages	£28,000
Machine repairs	£2,500
Entertaining UK customers	£1,400
Entertaining overseas customers	£900
Car to be used exclusively for business	£12,600

The above six expense amounts are stated inclusive of VAT where applicable.

Required:

Calculate the VAT payable for the quarter ended 31 March 2017 and state by when this amount must be paid.

43 DEFINITIONS

Nuala wishes to know a little more about VAT. You have offered to explain the meaning of taxable persons and taxable supplies to her.

Required:

(a) **What is a taxable person for VAT purposes?**

(b) **Name four conditions that must be met before a supply can come within the scope of VAT.**

44 BROADHURST

Broadhurst is in business and has been registered for VAT for several years. He has given you the following information to help you prepare his VAT return for the quarter ended 31 December 2016. All items are standard rated except where noted and are stated excluding VAT.

	£
Sales (Note 1)	175,560
Purchases of goods	113,670
Purchase returns	5,249
Purchase of a car (Note 2)	14,000
Entertaining overseas customers	1,560

In addition Broadhurst wishes to claim impaired debt relief on an eight month old debt which he has just written off. The debt is £1,760.

Note 1 – Broadhurst offers a prompt payment discount of 1% for payment within 30 days. During the quarter discounts were taken in respect of sales invoices of £131,670 (VAT exclusive).

Note 2 – The car is to be used by the managing director 60% privately.

Required:

Show how Broadhurst would account for VAT for the quarter ended 31 December 2016 by stating the figures that would be entered into the relevant boxes on the VAT return pro forma shown below.

Enter VAT figures including pence.

Box 1	VAT due in this period on sales and other outputs	
Box 4	VAT reclaimed in the period on purchases and other inputs	
Box 5	Net VAT to be paid to HM Revenue and Customs or reclaimed by you	
Box 6	Total value of sales and all other outputs excluding any VAT	
Box 7	Total value of purchases and all other inputs excluding any VAT	

45 DENZIL DYER

Denzil Dyer has been a self-employed printer since 2008. He has recently registered for value added tax (VAT). Denzil's sales consist of printed leaflets, some of which are standard rated and some of which are zero rated. He sells to both VAT registered customers and to non-VAT registered customers.

Customers making an order of more than £500 are given a discount of 5% from the normal selling price. Denzil also offers a discount of 2.5% of the amount payable to those customers that pay within one month of the date of the sales invoice.

All of Denzil's printing supplies are purchased from a VAT registered supplier. He pays by credit card and receives a VAT invoice. However, Denzil also purchases various office supplies by cash without receiving any invoices.

Denzil does not use the annual accounting scheme, the cash accounting scheme or the flat rate scheme.

Required:

(a) Explain why it is important for Denzil to correctly identify whether a sale is standard rated or whether it is zero rated.

(b) Explain the VAT implications of the two types of discount that Denzil gives.

(c) Advise Denzil of the conditions that will have to be met in order for him to recover input VAT. You are not expected to list those goods and services for which input VAT is non-recoverable.

(d) State the circumstances in which Denzil is and is not required to issue a VAT invoice, and the period during which such an invoice should be issued.

46 VARDY PLC

You are a trainee accountant working for the internal audit department of Vardy plc, an internet-based retail business.

For the previous three value added tax (VAT) quarters, Vardy plc has been late in submitting its VAT returns and in paying the related VAT liabilities. The company is therefore currently serving a default surcharge period.

As part of your department's tax audit for the year ended 31 March 2017, you have discovered that Vardy plc has been careless in incorrectly treating the supply of standard rated services received from VAT registered businesses situated elsewhere within the European Union. This careless incorrect treatment has resulted in an underpayment of VAT to HM Revenue and Customs of £8,200 for the year ended 31 March 2017.

Required:

(a) Advise Vardy plc of the default surcharge implications if during the current default surcharge period it is late in paying a further VAT liability, and what the company will need to do in order to revert to a clean default surcharge record.

(b) Explain why Vardy plc will be permitted to disclose the underpayment of VAT of £8,200 by entering this amount on its next VAT return, and state whether or not default interest will be due.

(c) Advise Vardy plc as to the maximum amount of penalty which is likely to be charged by HM Revenue and Customs in respect of the underpayment of VAT of £8,200, and by how much this penalty would be reduced as a result of the company's unprompted disclosure.

TASK 1.3

Assessment objective 3	Demonstrate an understanding of the inter-relationship between the financial accounting and management accounting systems of an organisation and how they can be used to support managers in decision making

47   NON-CURRENT ASSETS 1

NCA1 Limited is not registered for VAT and has a year end of 31 December 20X0.

The following is a purchase invoice received by NCA1 Limited:

	Invoice # 212532	
To: NCA1 Limited 428 Hoole Road Chester CH4 GFV	Graham's Garages 32 Oldfield Way Chester CH12 RTH	**Date:** 28 November X0
		£
Vauxhall Van Delivery Tax Disc	Registration number ES54 DCS	15,000.00 250.00 210.00
Less part exchange Amount due	Registration number FD01 VBA	(3,800.00) 11,660.00
Settlement terms: Strictly 60 days		

The following information relates to the vehicle that was part exchanged:

Registration number	FD01 VBA
Length of ownership	4 years 2 months
Purchase price	£12,000.00

- Vehicles are depreciated at 30% on a reducing balance basis.

- Non-current assets are depreciated in the year of acquisition but not in the year of disposal.

You now need to complete the journal to reflect the purchase of the new van and the part exchange of the old van.

Narrative	Dr	Cr
Totals		

48   NON-CURRENT ASSETS 2

- Dave's Doors is a sole trader business that is registered for VAT at the standard rate of 20%. His year end is 31/12/X4.

- During 20X4, machine 'A' was sold, for total proceeds of £10,000 (cheque received).

- Machine 'A' was acquired on 01/07/X1 at a cost of £20,000 (excluding VAT).

- The depreciation policy for machinery is 10% per annum on a reducing balance basis. Non-current assets are depreciated in full in the year of acquisition but not in the year of disposal.

(a)   What is the accumulated depreciation of machine 'A' in the year of disposal?

(b)   Complete the journal to reflect the disposal of machine 'A'. A picklist of account names has been provided below. You are able to use an account name more than once. More rows than required have been provided below.

Narrative	Dr	Cr
Totals		

Picklist: Machinery at cost account, Machinery accumulated depreciation account, Disposals account, VAT Control, Bank (accounts can be used more than once)

(c)   What was the profit or loss made on disposal?

49   YEAR-END 1

You are employed by Jane Parker who is a baker. You are her bookkeeper and she has asked you to create a trial balance. Below are the balances extracted from the main ledger at 30 April 20X2.

(a)   Enter the balances into the columns of the trial balance provided below. Total the two columns and enter an appropriate suspense account balance to ensure that the two totals agree.

	£	Debit	Credit
Accruals	4,820		
Prepayments	2,945		
Motor expenses	572		
Admin expenses	481		
Light and Heat	1,073		
Revenue	48,729		
Purchases	26,209		
SLCA	5,407		
PLCA	3,090		
Rent	45		
Purchase returns	306		
Discounts allowed	567		
Capital	10,000		
Loan	15,000		
Interest paid	750		
Drawings	4,770		
Motor vehicles – cost	19,000		
Motor vehicle – accumulated depreciation	2,043		
VAT control owing	2,995		
Wages	20,000		
Suspense account			
Totals			

(b)   Since the trial balance has been produced you have noticed a number of errors which are as follows:

   (i)   Jane put £5,000 into the business after receiving a large cheque as a Christmas present from her father. This has been put through the bank account but no other entries have been made.

   (ii)   The Gross column of the SDB has been overcast by £385.

   (iii)   The VAT column of the PDB has been undercast by £193.

   (iv)   An amount of £4,500 paid for rent has been credited to both the rent account and the bank account.

   (v)   An accrual for electricity at the year-end of £1,356 has been correctly credited to the accruals account but no other entry has been made.

Prepare the entries to correct these errors using the blank journal below. Dates and narratives are not required.

		Dr £	Cr
(i)			
(ii)			
(iii)			
(iv)			
(v)			

50   ETB 1

You work for Highland Ltd, a company that makes and sells parts for vintage cars. You have been provided with an ETB that has been started by the current bookkeeper. However, she is now on holiday and the owner of Highland Ltd has asked that you create the adjustments and enter them onto the ETB to save time.

Make the appropriate entries in the adjustments column of the extended trial balance to take account of the following. The year-end date is 31 December 20X5.

(a)   The allowances for doubtful debts figure is to be adjusted to 2% of receivables.

(b)   A credit note received from a supplier for goods returned was mislaid. It has since been found and has not yet been accounted for. It was for £2,000 net plus £400 VAT.

(c)   Rent is payable yearly in advance. For the 12 months to 31/10/X5 the rent is £12,000, the prepayment bought down has been included in the ledger balance. For the 12 months to 31/10/X6 the rent is £15,000.

(d)   Inventory is valued at cost at £14,890. However, there was a leak in the storage cupboard and £3,000 worth of items has been damaged and need to be written off.

(e)   The electricity bill of £450 for the 3 months ended 31 January 20X6 was received and paid in February 20X6.

Extended trial balance

Ledger account	Ledger balances		Adjustments	
	Dr £	Cr £	Dr £	Cr £
Accruals		1,330		
Advertising	1,800			
Bank	7,912			
Capital		50,000		
Closing inventory				
Depreciation charge				
Drawings	14,700			
Fixtures and fittings – accumulated depreciation		945		
Fixtures and fittings – cost	6,099			
Irrecoverable debts	345			
Allowance for doubtful debt adjustment				
Electricity	1,587			
Loan	10,000			
Opening inventory	5,215			
Prepayment				
Allowance for doubtful debts		485		
Purchases	78,921			
Purchase returns				
PLCA		14,000		
Rent	25,000			
Revenue		145,825		
SLCA	9,500			
VAT control account		11,453		
Wages	62,959			
	224,038	224,038		

51 ETB 2

You have the following extended trial balance. The adjustments have already been correctly entered. You now need to extend the figures into the statement of profit or loss and statement of financial position columns. Make the columns balance by entering figures and a label in the correct places.

Extended trial balance

Ledger account	Ledger balances		Adjustments		Statement of profit or loss		Statement of financial position	
	Dr £	Cr £	Dr £	Cr £	Dr £	Cr £	Dr £	Cr £
Accruals		2,300		425				
Advertising	1,800							
Bank	7,912		1,175					
Capital		40,000						
Closing inventory			6,590	6,590				
Depreciation charge			821					
Drawings	14,700							
Fixtures and fittings – accumulated depreciation		945		821				
Fixtures and fittings – cost	6,099							
Interest	345							
Light and heat	1,587		706					
Loan		10,000						
Opening inventory	5,215							
Prepayments	485		927	281				
Purchases	75,921							
PLCA		14,000						
Rent and rates	38,000			927				
Revenue		145,825						
SLCA	9,500			1,175				
VAT control account		11,453						
Wages	62,959							
	224,523	224,523	10,219	10,219				

52 INCOMPLETE 1

You are working on the accounts of Control Ltd for the year ended 30 September 20X6. You have the following information:

Sales for the year ended 30 September 20X6

- Credit sales amounted to £46,000 net of sales tax
- Cash sales amounted to £212,000 net of sales tax
- All sales are standard rated for sales tax at 20%.

Payments from the bank account for the year ended 30 September 20X6

- Payroll expenses   £48,000
- Administration expenses   £6,400 ignore sales tax
- Vehicle running costs   £192,000 including sales tax at 20%
- Drawings   £41,800
- Sales tax   £17,300

Summary of balances available

Balance as at	30 September 20X5	30 September 20X6
Bank account	5,630	8,140
Trade receivables	4,120	5,710
Sales tax (credit balances)	4,200	4,575

(a) Calculate the figure for credit sales for entry into the receivables (sales ledger) control account?

£_____

(b) Using the figures given above (including your answer to part (a), prepare the sales ledger control account for the year ended 30 September 20X6, showing clearly the receipts paid into the bank as the balancing figure.

Receivables (Sales ledger) control account

(c) Calculate the cash sales inclusive of sales tax which have been paid into the bank account. All cash sales are banked.

£_____

(d) **Show a summarised bank account for the year ended 30 September 20X6.**

Bank account

53 INCOMPLETE 2

You are given the following information about a sole trader called Brian as at 31 March 20X2:

The value of assets and liabilities were:

•	Non-current assets at carrying amount	£14,000
•	Bank	£2,500
•	Trade payables	£10,300
•	Opening capital (at 1 April 20X1)	£3,700
•	Drawings for the year	£1,500

There were no other assets or liabilities.

Calculate the profit for the year ended 30 March 20X2.

£_____

54 INCOMPLETE 3

During the year ended 30 September 20X7, Elsie, a sole trader, made sales of £1,280,000 and made a sales margin of 25% on these. Rosemary made purchases of £970,200 during the year ended 30 September 20X7 and inventory was valued at £98,006 at the period end.

Using this information, complete the following:

(a) **Calculate the cost of goods sold for the year ended 30 September 20X7.**

£_____

(b) **Calculate the value of the inventory at 1 October 20X6.**

£_____

55   SOLE TRADER 1

You have the following trial balance for a sole trader known as Vincent Trading. All the necessary year-end adjustments have been made.

Vincent Trading has a policy of showing trade receivables net of any allowance for doubtful debts and showing trade payables and sundry payables as one total figure.

The statement of profit or loss for Vincent Trading shows a profit of £8,810 for the period.

Prepare a statement of financial position for the business for the year ended 30 June 20X8.

Vincent Trading		
Trial balance as at 30 June 20X8		
	Dr **£**	**Cr** **£**
Accruals		750
Bank		1,250
Capital		17,000
Closing inventory	7,850	7,850
Discounts received		900
Sundry payables		1,450
Purchase ledger control account		6,800
Depreciation charge	1,600	
Discounts allowed	345	
Allowance for doubtful debts adjustment	295	
Equipment accumulated depreciation		4,500
Wages	24,000	
Sales ledger control account	7,800	
Rent	5,250	
Revenue		164,000
Disposal		450
Prepayments	3,200	
Purchases	125,000	
Sales returns	1,500	
Opening inventory	3,450	
Equipment at cost	17,500	
Drawings	8,000	
General expenses	2,950	
Allowance for doubtful debts		840
VAT		2,950
	208,740	208,740

Vincent Trading

Statement of financial position as at 30 June 20X8

	£	£	£
Non-current assets	Cost	Depreciation	Carrying amount
Current assets			
Current liabilities			
Net current assets			
Net assets			
Financed by:			
Opening capital			
Add:			
Less:			
Closing capital			

56   SOLE TRADER 2

You are preparing the statement of financial position for Beale, a sole trader. All the necessary year-end adjustments have been made.

Beale has a policy of showing trade receivables net of any allowance for doubtful debts. The statement of profit or loss for Beale shows a loss of £4,350 for the period.

Prepare a statement of financial position for the business for the year ended 30 June 20X6.

Beale – Trial balance as at 30 June 20X6		
	Dr £	Cr £
Accruals		3,150
Administration expenses	45,000	
Bank		2,250
Capital		85,000
Cash	500	
Closing inventory	17,500	17,500
Depreciation charge	9,000	
Disposal of non-current asset		1,500
Motor vehicles at cost	45,000	
Motor vehicles accumulated depreciation		20,000
Opening inventory	15,000	
Allowance for doubtful debts		1,450
Allowance for doubtful debts adjustment	200	
Purchases	75,000	
Purchases ledger control account		23,750
Revenue		130,000
Sales ledger control account	68,550	
Selling expenses	9,150	
Drawings	3,200	
VAT		3,500
Total	288,100	288,100

Beale – Statement of financial position as at 30 June 20X6			
	£	£	£
Non-current assets	Cost	Depreciation	Carrying amount
Current assets			
Current liabilities			
Net current assets			
Net assets			
Financed by:			
Opening capital			
Less:			
Less:			
Closing capital			

57 PARTNER 1

You have the following information about a partnership business:

The financial year ends on 30 June.

- The partners are Gertrude, Eddie and Polonius.

- Partners' annual salaries

    - Gertrude   £18,000

    - Eddie   nil

    - Polonius   £36,000

- Partners' interest on capital

    - Gertrude   £2,000 per annum

    - Eddie   £2,000 per annum

    - Polonius   £2,000 per annum

- Partners' sales commission earned during the year
  - Gertrude   £8,250
  - Eddie   £6,800
  - Polonius   £4,715
- Profit share
  - Gertrude   40%
  - Eddie   40%
  - Polonius   20%

The statement of profit or loss for the partnership shows a profit for the year ended 30 June 20X9 of £220,000 before appropriations.

Prepare the appropriation account for the partnership for the year ended 30 June 20X9. Enter zeros where appropriate and use minus signs for deductions.

Partnership appropriation account for the year ended 30 June 20X9

	£
Profit for the year	
Salaries:	
Gertrude	
Eddie	
Polonius	
Interest on capital:	
Gertrude	
Eddie	
Polonius	
Sales commission:	
Gertrude	
Eddie	
Polonius	
Profit available for distribution	

Profit share:	
Gertrude	
Eddie	
Polonius	
Total residual profit distributed	

58   PARTNER 2

You have the following information about a partnership:

- The partners are Cordelia and Goneril, and the partnership produces luxury gifts for Fathers' Day and other special occasions.

- Regan joined the partnership on 1 May 20X7 when she introduced £128,000 into the business bank account.

- Profit share, effective until 30 April 20X7

    –   Cordelia   35%

    –   Goneril   65%

- Profit share, effective from 1 May 20X7

    –   Cordelia   25%

    –   Goneril   45%

    –   Regan   30%

- Goodwill was valued at £105,000 on 30 April 20X7.

- Goodwill is to be introduced into the partners' capital accounts on 30 April and then eliminated on 1 May.

(a)   **Show the entries required to introduce the goodwill into the partnership accounting records.**

Account name	Dr	Cr

Cordelia is thinking of leaving the partnership next year. It is estimated that Regan's good reputation will have added £22,000 to the goodwill value by then.

(b)   **Calculate the goodwill to be introduced into Cordelia's capital account at the time of her departure.**

£_____

59   PARTNER 3

Macbeth, Hamlet and Will are in partnership selling cases for mobile phones.

- Will retired from the partnership on 30 June 20X5. He has agreed that the partnership will pay what he is due from the bank account in full.

- Profit share, effective until 30 June 20X5

    –   Macbeth   30%

    –   Hamlet   40%

    –   Will   30%

- Profit share, effective from 1 July 20X5

  – Macbeth 50%

  – Hamlet 50%

- Goodwill was valued at £50,000 on 30 June 20X5.

- Goodwill is to be introduced into the partners' capital accounts on 30 June and then eliminated on 1 July.

- At the 30 June 20X5 the partners had the following balances on their capital and current accounts:

  – Macbeth £7,000 (capital a/c) and £11,000 (current a/c)

  – Hamlet £8,000 (capital a/c) and £9,000 (current a/c)

  – Will £9,000 (capital a/c) and £7,000 (current a/c)

Prepare the capital account for Will, showing clearly the transfer from the current account and the amount paid to Will on his retirement.

Capital account – Will

		Balance b/d	9,000

60 COSTING 1

The inventory record for component XYZ for the month of January showed:

	Receipts	Value £	Issues
Opening inventory	500	1,250	
4 January	1,000	2,750	
11 January	1,600	4,480	
18 January	1,200	3,480	
19 January			2,100
25 January	1,500	4,350	
31 January			1,800

(a) **Calculate the cost of issues during the month using the FIFO method of pricing issues.**

(b) **Calculate the value of inventory at 31 January using the LIFO method of pricing issues.**

(c) **Calculate the price at which the issues on 31 January would be made using the cumulative weighted average cost method of pricing.**

61   COSTING 2

Which method of inventory valuation is being described?

Characteristic	FIFO	LIFO	AVCO
Potentially out of date valuation on issues.			
The valuation of inventory rarely reflects the actual purchase price of the material.			
Potentially out of date closing inventory valuation.			
This inventory valuation method is particularly suited to inventory that consist of liquid materials e.g. oil.			
This inventory valuation method is particularly suited to inventory that has a short shelf life e.g. dairy products.			
This inventory valuation method is suited to a wheat farmer who has large silos of grain. Grain is added to and taken from the top of these silos.			
In times of rising prices this method will give higher profits.			
In times of rising prices this method will give lower profits.			
In times of rising prices this method gives a middle level of profits compared to the other two.			
Issues are valued at the most recent purchase cost.			
Inventory is valued at the average of the cost of purchases.			
Inventory is valued at the most recent purchase cost.			

62   COSTING 3

How would the following labour costs be classified?

Cost	Direct	Indirect
Basic pay for production workers		
Supervisors wages		
Bonus for salesman		
Production workers overtime premium due to general pressures		
Holiday pay for production workers		
Sick pay for supervisors		
Time spent by production workers cleaning the machinery		

63   COSTING 4

A company employs a group of production workers who, as well as earning basic pay, are also paid a weekly group bonus based on their productivity during each week.

The group has a standard (target) output of 800 units of production per hour worked. All output in excess of this level earns a bonus for each of the employees.

The bonus % is calculated as:

$$25\% \times \frac{\text{Excess production (units)}}{\text{Standard production (units)}} \times 100$$

The bonus rate per hour is then calculated as: bonus % × £10.

The following information relates to this group's performance last week:

	Hours worked	Actual production (units)
Monday	920	940,000
Tuesday	870	890,000
Wednesday	910	930,000
Thursday	920	960,000
Friday	940	990,000
Saturday	440	690,000
Total	5,000	5,400,000

(a)   **Use the table below to calculate the group bonus rate per hour and the total bonus to be paid to the group.**

	Units
Actual production	
Less standard production (based on actual hours worked)	
Excess production	
Bonus %	
Group bonus rate per hour £	
Total group bonus £	

(b)   **An employee in this group worked for 44 hours last week, and is paid a basic rate of £9.60 per hour. The employee's total pay for last week was:**

£

64 COSTING 5

The coating department of JH Holdings Ltd uses process costing for coating metal components with a hard layer of titanium nitride to increase longevity.

The process account for January for one particular process has been partly completed but the following information is also relevant:

Four employees worked on this process during January. Each employee worked 30 hours per week for 4 weeks and was paid £12 per hour.

Overheads are absorbed on the basis of £8 per labour hour.

JH Holdings Ltd expects a normal loss of 10% during this process, which it then sells for scrap at £5 per kg.

Complete the process account below for January.

Description	Units	Unit cost £	Total cost £	Description	Units	Unit cost £	Total cost £
Input – components	300	11.25	3,375	Normal loss		5.00	
Materials – coating			500	Output	290		
Labour							
Overheads							

65 COSTING 6

Silver makes key rings on a production line. Details of the process in period 2 are as follows:

OWIP = 250 units

Costs incurred so far

	Materials	£53,800
	Conversion	£42,000

Degrees of completion

	Materials	100%
	Conversion	60%

Completed output = 3,200 units

Costs incurred in Period 2:

	Materials	£135,000
	Conversion	£98,800

Calculate the cost per equivalent unit using the AVCO method of valuing WIP.

Equivalent units	Material	Conversion
Cost per EU		

66   OVERHEADS 1

National Coaches Ltd (NCL) runs a fleet of coaches and buses, operating across the country. Some services are scheduled but many others are chartered by specific organisations – for example, running school buses for taking students to and from school.

NCL has budgeted for the following overheads for its two profit and three cost centres for quarter 1 of the next financial year:

	£000	£000
Depreciation of vehicles		36,400
Fuel and other variable costs		42,200
Driver salaries:		
Scheduled routes	5,250	
Chartered services	4,709	
Total driver salaries		9,959
Rent and rates and other premises costs		12,600
Indirect labour costs:		
Bus maintenance and repairs	9,600	
Fuel and parts store	3,200	
General administration	7,800	
Total indirect labour cost		20,600

The following information is also available:

Profit/cost centre	NBV of vehicles (£000)	Planned mileage	Floor space (m²)	Number of employees
Scheduled routes	1,080,000	215,600		105
Chartered services	720,000	176,400		96
Vehicle maintenance and repairs			190,000	260
Fuel and parts store			114,000	146
General administration			76,000	220
Total	1,800,000	392,000	380,000	827

Primary allocations/apportionments are made on the most appropriate basis. The support cost centres are then reapportioned to the two profit centres using the direct method.

- The vehicle maintenance and repairs cost centre spends 60% of its time maintaining the buses in the scheduled routes profit centre and the remainder in the chartered services profit centre.

- 55% of the issues from the Fuel and parts store cost centre are made to the scheduled routes profit centre and the remainder in the chartered services profit centre.

- The scheduled routes profit centre and the chartered services profit centre both incur general administration costs equally.

- The three support cost centres are not involved in reciprocal servicing.

Use the following table to allocate or apportion the overheads between the profit/cost centres, using the most appropriate basis.

	Basis of apportionment	Scheduled routes £000	Chartered Services £000	Vehicle maintenance and repairs £000	Fuel and parts store £000	General admin. £000	Totals £000
Depreciation of vehicles							
Fuel and other variable costs							
Driver salaries							
Rent and rates and other premises costs							
Indirect labour							
Totals							
Reapportion vehicle maintenance and repairs							
Reapportion Fuel and parts store							
Reapportion General admin.							
Total overheads to profit centres							

67 OVERHEADS 2

The ABC Company manufactures two products, Product Alpha and Product Beta. Both are produced in a very labour-intensive environment and use similar processes. Alpha and Beta differ by volume. Beta is a high-volume product, while Alpha is a low-volume product. Details of product inputs, outputs and the costs of activities are as follows:

	Direct labour hours/unit	Annual output (units)	Number of purchase orders	Number of set-ups
Alpha	5	1,200	70	40
Beta	5	10,800	80	60
			150	100

Fixed overhead costs amount to a total of £420,000 and have been analysed as follows:

	£
Labour-related	90,000
Purchasing related	150,000
Set-up related	180,000

(a) Using a traditional method of overhead absorption based on labour hours, what is the overhead cost per unit for each unit of product Alpha?

(b) Using a traditional method of overhead absorption based on labour hours, what is the overhead cost per unit for each unit of product Beta?

(c) Using Activity Based Costing as method of overhead absorption, what is the overhead cost per unit for each unit of product Alpha?

(d) Using Activity Based Costing as method of overhead absorption, what is the overhead cost per unit for each unit of product Beta?

68 OVERHEADS 3

Animal Feeds Ltd has prepared a forecast for the next quarter for organic animal feed.

Animal Feeds Ltd budgets to produce 1,800 kg of the feed and sell 1,000 kg. The cost and revenue for this budget is as follows:

	£000
Sales	50,000
Direct materials	7,560
Direct labour	17,640
Fixed production overheads	3,600
Advertising (fixed cost)	2,010

Animal Feeds Ltd has no opening inventory of the feed.

Produce a marginal costing statement of profit or loss and an absorption costing statement of profit or loss:

Marginal costing	£000	£000
Sales		
Opening inventory		
Production costs		
Less: Closing inventory		
Less: Cost of sales		
Contribution		
Less: Fixed costs		
Profit for the period		

Absorption costing	£000	£000
Sales		
Opening inventory		
Production costs		
Less: Closing inventory		
Less: Cost of sales		
Gross profit		
Less: Non-production cost		
Profit for the period		

69 DECISIONS 1

John Robertson, a self-employed builder, has been asked to provide a fixed price quotation for some building work required by a customer. Robertson's accountant has compiled the following figures, together with some notes as a basis for a quotation.

		£	
Direct materials:			
Bricks	200,000 at $100 per thousand	20,000	Note 1
	200,000 at $120 per thousand	24,000	
Other materials		5,000	Note 2
Direct labour:			
Skilled	3,200 hours at $12 per hour	38,400	Note 3
Unskilled	2,000 hours at $6 per hour	12,000	Note 4
Other costs:			
Scaffolding hire		3,500	Note 5
Depreciation of general purpose machinery		2,000	Note 6
General overheads 5,200 hours at $1 per hour		5,200	Note 7
Plans		2,000	Note 8
		———	
Total cost		112,100	
Profit		22,420	Note 9
		———	
Suggested price		134,520	
		———	

Notes:

(1) The contract requires 400,000 bricks, 200,000 are already in inventory and 200,000 will have to be bought in. This is a standard type of brick regularly used by Robertson. The 200,000 in inventory were purchased earlier in the year at £100 per 1,000. The current replacement cost of this type of brick is £120 per 1,000. If the bricks in inventory are not used on this job John is confident that he will be able to use them later in the year.

(2) Other materials will be bought in as required; this figure represents the purchase price.

(3) All skilled labour will be hired on an hourly basis. The current cost of skilled workers is £12 per hour.

(4) John employs four unskilled workers on contracts guaranteeing them a 40 hour week at £6 per hour. These unskilled labourers are currently idle and would have sufficient spare time to complete the proposal under consideration.

(5) This is the estimated cost of hiring scaffolding.

(6) John estimates that the project will take 20 weeks to complete. This represents 20 weeks' straight line depreciation on equipment used. If the equipment is not used on this job it will stand idle for the 20 week period. In either case its value at the end of the 20-week period will be identical.

(7) This represents the rental cost of John's storage yard. If he does not undertake the above job he can rent his yard out to a competitor who will pay him rent of £500 per week for the 20-week period.

(8) This is the cost of the plans that John has already had drawn for the project.

(9) John attempts to earn a mark-up of 20% on cost on all work undertaken.

John is surprised at the suggested price and considers it rather high. He knows that there will be a lot of competition for the work.

Required:

Using relevant costing principles, calculate the lowest price that John could quote for the customer's building work. Explain your treatment of each item in the accountant's estimate.

70   DECISIONS 2

Dilemma makes a product that is aimed at the teenage leisure market in the UK. After a number of successful years they are considering whether to expand their production capability by a factor of 50% to take advantage of rising demand. The accountant has produced the following information:

(1)   Current sales per year – 500,000 units at £1.70 per unit.

(2)   Variable costs £1.40 per unit.

(3)   Fixed costs £96,000 per year.

(4)   If production is increased it is anticipated that:

(i)   fixed costs will increase by £34,000

(ii)   variable costs are expected to fall by £0.05 per unit due to bulk purchasing of raw material

(iii)   the selling price is expected to fall by £0.10 per unit for all units.

At a recent management meeting the following comments were noted:

(1)   The Production Director expressed concern at the revenue projections. In his opinion there are a number of risks inherent in the new strategy. His main concern is that the total number of teenagers is falling, although he conceded that perhaps future teenagers may have more money to spend per head. He also asked if future changes in raw material prices and wage rates had been fully taken into account.

(2)   The Sales Director stated that she felt much more confident about the plan and said that sales had been rising for some time and, in her opinion, the number of teenagers is increasing. She also thought that inflation should not be too much of a problem.

Required:

(a)   For both the present and proposed situations calculate:

(i)   the breakeven point in units and sales revenue

(ii)   the annual profit

(iii)   the margin of safety ratio.

(b)   On the basis of your answers to part (a), state, with reasons, what your advice would be to Dilemma.

71 DECISIONS 3

(a) X manufactures four liquids – A, B, C and D. The selling price and unit cost details for these products are as follows:

	A	B	C	D
	£/litre	£/litre	£/litre	£/litre
Selling price	100	110	120	120
Direct materials	24	30	16	21
Direct labour ($6/hour)	18	15	24	27
Direct expenses	–	–	3	–
Variable overhead	12	10	16	18
Fixed overhead (Note 1)	24	20	32	36
Profit	22	35	29	18

Note 1:

Fixed overhead is absorbed on the basis of labour hours, based on a budget of 1,600 hours per quarter.

During the next three months the number of direct labour hours is expected to be limited to 1,345. The same labour is used for all products.

The marketing director has identified the maximum demand for each of the four products during the next three months as follows:

A   200 litres

B   150 litres

C   100 litres

D   120 litres

These maximum demand levels include the effects of a contract already made between X and one of its customers, Y, to supply 20 litres of each of A, B, C and D during the next three months.

You are required to determine the number of litres of products A, B, C and D to be produced/sold in the next three months in order to maximise profits, and calculate the profit that this would yield.

Assume that no inventory is held at the beginning of the three months which may be used to satisfy demand in the period.

72 DECISIONS 4

One of the polishing machines in Greg Ltd's polishing department is nearing the end of its useful life and the company is considering purchasing a replacement machine.

Estimates have been made for the initial capital cost, sales income and operating costs of the replacement machine, which is expected to have a useful life of three years:

	Year 0 £000	Year 1 £000	Year 2 £000	Year 3 £000
Capital expenditure	500			
Other cash flows:				
Sales income		280	330	370
Operating costs		100	120	140

The company appraises capital investment projects using a 10% cost of capital.

(a) **Complete the table below and calculate the net present value of the proposed replacement machine (to the nearest £000).**

	Year 0 £000	Year 1 £000	Year 2 £000	Year 3 £000
Capital expenditure				
Sales income				
Operating costs				
Net cash flows				
PV factors	1.0000	0.909	0.826	0.751
Discounted cash flows				
Net present value				

The net present value is *positive/negative**

delete as appropriate

(b) **Estimate the IRR of this project**

A 0%

B 5%

C 10%

D 15%

(c) **Calculate the payback of the proposed replacement machine to the nearest whole month.**

TASK 1.4

Assessment objective 4	Apply ethical and accounting principles when preparing final accounts for different types of organisation, develop ethical courses of action and communicate relevant information effectively

73   AVOIDANCE

As part of the year end accounting procedures the Finance Director of Void Ltd is estimating the likely tax liability. As well as incorporating the finalised profit figure, the team involved are also looking at different ways of reducing the tax bill.

You are concerned that some of these methods may constitute tax evasion rather than tax avoidance.

Required:

Which of the following statements correctly explains the difference between tax evasion and tax avoidance?

Both tax evasion and tax avoidance are illegal, but tax evasion involves providing HM Revenue and Customs with deliberately false information.	
Tax evasion is illegal, whereas tax avoidance involves the minimisation of tax liabilities by the use of any lawful means.	
Both tax evasion and tax avoidance are illegal, but tax avoidance involves providing HM Revenue and Customs with deliberately false information.	
Tax avoidance is illegal, whereas tax evasion involves the minimisation of tax liabilities by the use of any lawful means.	

74   DUMPING

During your lunch you read an article in the FT about a case where a company was prosecuted through the courts for a breach of environmental laws regarding the dumping of toxic waste into drains, which subsequently lead to the open ocean. The case included testimony from the company's auditors which secured the prosecution.

You discussed this with one of the juniors who said that she thought that this would constitute a breach of confidentiality on behalf of the auditor.

Required:

Explain why this is not the case.

75   INTEGRITY

Frankie is an AAT member working for Lightfoots Ltd as an assistant to the management accountant. His finance director has asked him to post a journal to transfer £20,000, a material sum, out of maintenance costs and into non-current assets, thus boosting profit for the period. Frankie has checked the details and feels that there is no justification for the journal.

Required:

Explain what Frankie should do, highlighting both internal and external courses of action.

76 BENEFITS

Jacqui has recently been appointed as the chief accountant for a small public sector organisation. The other members of the senior management team (SMT) are very pleased with her appointment as they have really struggled to attract, recruit and retain good staff.

At the last meeting of the SMT it was decided that the benefits package for senior staff (including the SMT) was inadequate and that it needed revising.

Jacqui was asked to draw up the new package and, after considerable research and benchmarking, has decided that a significant increase is needed in the benefits package.

Required:

(a) Discuss which ethical principles are potentially compromised here.

(b) Identify which factors Jacqui should consider before making a decision what to do.

(c) Explain what the best course of action would be.

77 SUSHIL

Sushil is a member in business. His manager has asked him to falsify the accounts and has made it clear that if he refuses then he will lose his job.

Required:

(a) State which type of threat this situation represents.

(b) Explain what the best course of action would be.

78 TRUE

Naill is an AAT member working for a large building company. The finance director has asked him to adjust some of the sales figures, so that the year-end final numbers look better than they actually are.

Required:

(a) Discuss whether Naill should do as the Finance Director instructs?

(b) Explain what is mean by 'false accounting'.

79 MEERA

Meera works for a large accountancy firm as a tax specialist. Recently two matters have arisen:

Matter 1

On Monday Meera was in a meeting with a potential new client.

The potential client started by stating that he felt Meera's fees proposal was far too high and she needed to reduce them substantially.

He then said that he believed his tax bill for the previous year was also too high but if Meera guaranteed to reduce his tax bill, then he would come to her firm.

Meera had a quick look at the figures and she believed the sum looked reasonable.

(a) Explain what Meera should do in response to the client's requests.

Matter 2

On Tuesday Meera had a dispute with Greg, a new client. After analysing Greg's tax affairs Meera had found a material error in the previous year's tax return that resulted in an underpayment of tax. The previous tax computations were prepared by Greg's previous accountant.

Meera advised Greg to tell HMRC about the error but so far he has refused to do so, claiming it is 'their problem, not his'.

(b)   Should Meera tell HRMC about the error?

(c)   What should Meera do if Greg continues to refuse to inform the HMRC?

80   RS

RS, an employee, prepares monthly management accounting information for XYZ which includes detailed performance data that is used to calculate staff bonuses. Based on information prepared by RS this year's bonuses will be lower than expected.

RS has had approaches from other staff offering various incentives to make accruals for additional revenue and other reversible adjustments, to enable all staff (including RS) to receive increased or higher bonuses.

(a)   Which two ethical principles are threatened here?

(b)   What type of ethical threat does RS face?

81   DISMISS

Sarah, a member employed in a division of a large building company, believes that one of the contract managers is attempting to short-cut building regulations by using substandard building materials in a new school.

Sarah has spoken to an internal whistle-blowing helpline about the situation and now the divisional manager is threatening to have her dismissed 'for not being a team player'.

Explain whether or not Sarah is protected by the PIDA (1998)?

82   SUSTENANCE

At a recent Board meeting of Sustenance plc the topic of sustainability arose. The main view given was that attempts to incorporate sustainability would inevitably increase costs and reduce profits. When the Finance Director tried to explain that this was not the case, the Marketing Director commented that sustainability was nothing to do with accountants anyway.

Required:

(a)   Outline the roles of professional accountants in contributing to sustainability.

(b)   Describe three ways in which an increased emphasis on sustainability can result in improved profits for a firm.

83 TIO RINO

Tio Rino is a global mining company that has received much criticism in the past over its sustainability record. Press coverage has focussed on environmental damage, pollution, labour and human rights abuses and deforestation as well as criticism that Tio Rino mines coal (which contributes to global warming when burnt) and uranium (which contributes to concerns over nuclear power).

However, on its website the firm states the following:

'Our business is sustainably finding, mining and processing mineral resources.'

Required:

FOR EACH of the Triple Bottom Line reporting headings suggest TWO ways that a mining company such as Tio Rino can be a sustainable mining company.

84 HOGGS FURNITURE

Jacob is a professional accountant working for Hoggs Furniture Ltd ('Hoggs'), a furniture manufacturer that supplies many high street retailers.

Matter

At the last management meeting it was announced that a major client of the company was threatening to terminate their contract with Hoggs unless it could demonstrate a clear commitment to sustainability. The team were unclear what this meant for Hoggs and asked Jacob to investigate further.

Required:

(a) **Explain what is meant by 'sustainability'.**

(b) **Explain FOUR areas that Jacob should appraise in order to answer the client's concerns.**

(c) **List THREE other ways Jacob can contribute to sustainability as an accountant.**

85 MLC

MLC is a clothing retailer who imports clothes from diverse suppliers worldwide. MLC has a very strong, well-publicised corporate ethical code. The company accountant has just found out that one of MLC suppliers use child labour in the manufacture of their clothes and pay very low wages with cramped, dangerous conditions. This is in breach of contract conditions with that supplier.

This was raised at the last Board meeting and a wide range of opinions were discussed, including the following:

- "Place more orders with the supplier – it's cheap labour so the margins are good, which should keep the shareholders happy."

- "Leave things as they are and hope the information doesn't get out."

- "Continue trading with the supplier but investigate the claims quietly."

- "Cancel all contracts with the supplier and release a press statement stating how the company will always act quickly and decisively if unethical practices are suspected."

Advise the board.

86 STEPHANIE

Stephanie has worked in the finance department of Alpha for 5 years and has been promoted to work alongside the management accountant. Stephanie is currently working towards an AAT qualification.

The AAT-qualified management accountant of Alpha has told Stephanie that he works closely with department heads to produce their annual budgets. He is happy to allow significant 'slack' to be built in to these budgets to make them easier to achieve since, in his view, this makes Alpha a much more relaxed place to work.

Following this conversation, Stephanie overheard the management accountant agreeing to alter budgeted production figures to make them easier to achieve in return for tickets to a major football game. When she questioned her boss, he told her no harm was done since the budgeted figures are subjective anyway.

Discuss which ethical principles the management accountant is in breach of?

87 STEVEN

As financial controller Steven has been asked to sign off N&Q Ltd's year-end accounts. He joined the company only three months ago.

The accounts include a note that is incorrect. Having investigated the matter, Steven recognises that this is a genuine mistake and not a deliberate attempt to mislead.

The Managing Director does not want to produce new accounts because of its inherent cost, but Steven does not feel it appropriate that he signs off something that has an error in it.

What action should Steven take?

Section 2

EXAM – PART II – PRACTICE TASKS

NOTE: Rather than splitting tasks by learning outcome, this section has a number of scenarios covering different aspects of the syllabus.

The answers to the tasks in these scenarios can be found as spreadsheet files on your MyKaplan account (together with the text and word files required).

Please go to www.mykaplan.co.uk and login using your username and password.

SCENARIO 1

SLICK PARTZ

You are an Accounting Technician working for the UK Branch of a company called **Slick Partz**. Your branch is a franchise of the parent company which is based in Europe. Slick Partz manufactures parts for hospital equipment at its factory in main land Europe and these are then sold to franchisees. The franchise is then responsible for selling the parts to hospitals in its sales area.

The franchise buys the parts from the parent company in Euros (€) but sells to the hospitals in GB Pounds (£).

You have been sent a file in text format by your Managing Director and he wants you to carry out some work on it using a spreadsheet package. The text file can be found on MyKaplan in Practise, Revision Material, Exam Kit Additional Resources. The text file will need to be downloaded and saved before starting the tasks.

Required:

TASK 1

(a)   Open a blank workbook.

(b)   Import the data found in the 'Slick Partz' text file into Sheet 1/ cell $A$1.

(c)   In Column D format the 'Cost_Price' as currency. It should be formatted as Euros (€ 123) to 2 decimal places.

(d)   In Column E format the 'Sales_Price' as currency. It should be formatted to GB Pounds to 2 decimal places.

(e)   Rename Sheet 1 as 'Data Import'.

(f)   Copy the 'Data Import' worksheet to a new worksheet in the same workbook and name it as Subtotals.

(g)   Set the page orientation to portrait and fit the data to the width of one page.

(h)   Save the workbook as 'Slick Partz'.

TASK 2

(a)   Sort the data in the 'Subtotals' worksheet in preparation for carrying out subtotalling. The subtotals that are needed are for Model and Tele_Sales_Operative.

(b)   Create subtotals for Model, summing the Sales quantity.

(c)   Create a further subtotal for Tele_Sales_Operative, summing the Sales quantity.

(d)   Convert the worksheet to show formulas.

(e)   Set the page orientation to landscape.

(f)   Save the workbook.

TASK 3

(a)   Create a new worksheet called 'Currency Conversion'.

(b)   Return to the 'Data Import' worksheet and Auto-Filter the data.

(c)   Filter by sales operative 'Monty Video'.

(d)   Copy the result and paste it into Cell A1 in the currency conversion worksheet.

(e)   Return to the 'Data Import' worksheet and remove the 'Monty Video' filter.

(f)   Save the workbook.

TASK 4

(a)   Open the 'Currency Conversion' worksheet.

(b)   Insert 3 rows at the top of the worksheet.

(c)   Insert a new column into Column 'E'.

(d)   In Cell D1, type Conversion Rate.

(e)   Make the font bold and underline the text. Format D1 to Right Justified.

(f)   Format Cell E1 to number to 2 decimal places and type 0.84.

(g)   In Cell E4 type Cost_Price_GBP (£).

(h)   Make the font bold in cells A4:I4.

(i)   Autofit column widths.

(j)   In Cell E5:E26 create a formula that converts the content of Cell D5:D26 to GBP (£) using the conversion rate in Cell E1.

(k)   Format Cells E5:E26 to GBP (£), to 2 decimal places.

(l)   Copy the currency conversion worksheet to another worksheet within the Slick Partz workbook and rename the new worksheet as Profit Calculation.

(m)   Return to the currency conversion worksheet and show formulas and auto fit the column widths.

(n)   Set the page orientation to landscape.

(o)   Save the workbook.

TASK 5

(a)   Open the 'Profit Calculation' worksheet.

(b)   In Cells J4, K4 and L4 create 3 new headings of 'Total Cost', 'Total Revenue' and 'Profit'. Use the same format as on earlier headings.

(c)   In Cell J5:J26 create a formula that multiplies Cost_Price_GBP (£) by Sales Quantity.

(d)   In Cell K5:K26 create a formula that multiplies Sales Price by Sales Quantity.

(e)   In Cell L5:L26 create a formula that calculates Profit (Total Revenue – Total Cost).

(f)   In Cell J29 create a formula that calculates the average Cost, do the same for Total Revenue and Profit in adjacent cells. Create a suitable heading in I29.

(g)   In Cell J30:L30 create formulas that calculate the largest number in each of the data sets. Create a suitable heading in I30.

(h)   In Cell J31:L31 create formulas that calculate the smallest number in each of the data sets. Create a suitable heading in I31.

(i)   Show formulas and auto-fit column widths.

(j)   Set the page orientation to landscape, and move the page break to the left of column I.

(k)   Save the workbook.

TASK 6

(a)   Open the Data Import worksheet.

(b)   Using the data create a Pivot Table in a new worksheet that shows the quantity of each individual model sold by each sales operative.

(c)   Rename the worksheet 'Pivot' and move it to the right of the Profit Calculation sheet.

(d)   Remove Grand Totals for Rows and Columns.

(e)   Create a Pivot Chart and locate it on the Pivot worksheet. The type of chart should be a Clustered Column Chart. Add a suitable title to the chart.

(f)   Add Customer as a Page Field.

(g)   Save the workbook.

TASK 7

(a)   Create a new Worksheet and rename it 'Product Lookup'.

(b)   In cell A2 type "Product Code", font size 12 and bold. In cell B2 create a list of product codes from the data import worksheet using Data Validation.

(c)   In cell A6 type "Cost Price", font size 12 and bold. Format cell B6 to have a border, grey fill, bold size 12 font and currency € Euro (€123) to 2 decimal places.

(d)   In cell A9 type "Stock quantity", font size 12 and bold. Format Cells B9 and B12 to have a border, a grey fill and bold size 12 font.

(e)   In cell B6 create a VLOOKUP to look up the Product-Code chosen in Cell B2 in the Data Import worksheet and return the Cost_Price. The VLOOKUP should be set to look for only exact matches.

(f)   By adding an IF statement to the VLOOKUP in cell B6 ensure that if cell B2 is empty then cell B6 remains empty, if B2 contains a product code the VLOOKUP should return the cost price.

(g)   In cell B9 create a VLOOKUP to look up the Product-Code chosen in Cell B2 in the Data Import worksheet and return the Stock_Quantity. The VLOOKUP should be set to look for only exact matches.

(h)   By adding an IF statement to the VLOOKUP in cell B9 ensure that if cell B2 is empty then cell B9 remains empty, if B2 contains a product code the VLOOKUP should return the stock quantity.

(i)   In Cell B12, create a formula that produces the word "Re-order" if the value in Cell B9 is greater than 0 and less than 20.

(j)   Set Conditional Formatting to Cell B2 so that the cell has a bright yellow fill when something is entered into the cell.

(k)   Set Conditional Formatting to Cell B6 and B9 so that the cell has a black fill and white text when something is entered into the Cell B2.

(l)   Set Conditional Formatting to Cell B12 so that the cell has a black fill and white text when the value of B9 is greater than 0 but less than 20.

(m)   Show formulas and Autofit column widths.

(n)   Set page orientation to 'Landscape'.

(o)   Save the workbook.

TASK 8

(a)   Add a header to each worksheet, in the central box put in the name of each worksheet (as shown on each tab).

(b)   Add a footer to each worksheet, in the left hand box put your name and AAT registration number and in the right hand box put the date.

(c)   Save the workbook.

SCENARIO 2

BETTABAKE

You work for a small bakery. They are very good at making cakes but not very good at doing their budgets. They are constantly running out of material because they do not predict accurately what cakes they are going to make that day.

The company makes four different cakes.

The Whirl

Splash

Butterbun

Chocco

Ingredient requirements for each product are:

Cake	Eggs	Flour	Sugar	Butter	Cream
The Whirl	1	50g	35g	28g	12g
Splash	1.5	30g	18g	22g	10g
Butterbun	2	65g	27g	24g	0
Chocco	1	55g	30g	21g	0

The following information is also available with regards to costs:

Ingredient	Quantity	Total cost
Eggs	12	£1.50
Flour	200g	£1.80
Sugar	200g	£2.20
Butter	1000g	£6.00
Cream	300g	£2.50

Required:

The Production Manager wants you to prepare a spreadsheet workbook that will help her with her budgets.

TASK 1

Set up a new workbook. The workbook will need 4 worksheets.

Rename:

Worksheet 1	Ingredients
Worksheet 2	Cost per unit
Worksheet 3	Cost per cake
Worksheet 4	Budget

Save the workbook as 'Bettabake'

TASK 2

On the 'Ingredients' worksheet:

(a)   Starting in Cell A1 input the ingredient requirements for each cake, found at the start of this scenario. Making sure you include the column and row headings.

(b)   Format row and column headings in bold.

(c)   Save your work.

TASK 3

On the 'Cost per unit' worksheet, starting in Cell A1:

(a)   Create a spreadsheet that will calculate the cost per unit of ingredients. Four columns will be required:

      (i)   Ingredients (Column A).

      (ii)   Total Cost (Column B) – format as currency £ to 2 decimal places.

      (iii)   No of Units (Column C) – format as number to 0 decimal places.

      (iv)   Cost per Unit (Column D) – format as currency £ to 3 decimal places.

(b)   Input the cost data found in the scenario into columns B and C.

(c)   Use a formula in column D to calculate the cost per ingredient i.e. per egg or per gram.

TASK 4

On the 'Cost per cake' worksheet, starting at Cell A1:

(a)   Set up a spreadsheet to calculate the cost per cake. Ingredients should be the column titles and cake type row titles.

(b)   Using the 'Ingredients' worksheet and the 'Cost per unit' worksheet create formulas in cells B2 to F5 that will calculate the total cost of each ingredient for each cake. Give consideration to where absolute and relative referencing will be required.

(c)   Add a column for 'Total Cost per Cake'.

(d)   Format all cells as currency £ to 3 decimal places.

(e)   Show formulas and auto-fit column widths.

(f)   Set the page orientation to landscape.

(g)   Save your work.

TASK 5

On the 'Budget' worksheet you need to create a spreadsheet so the Production Director can type in any quantity of each cake and the spreadsheet will calculate how much of each ingredient is required.

(a)   Starting in Cell A3 you will need to create a row for each cake. Cells B3 to B6 will be used by the Production Director to input the quantity of cakes. Provide a suitable heading for cells B3 to B6 in cell B2.

(b)   Format the headings to bold and put a thick box border around the table.

(c)   Starting in Cell B11 you will need a column heading for each type of ingredient. In the cells beneath these headings create a formula that calculates the quantity of ingredients required to manufacture the volume of cakes entered in Column B. This will use the Ingredients worksheet. Use absolute referencing where necessary.

(d)   Add a row at the bottom of the table for totals for each ingredient, use a function to calculate the totals. Provide a title for this row in cell A16.

(e)   Format the headings to bold and put a thick box border around the table. Format the values in the table to 'accounting'.

(f)   Add a row at the bottom of the table to calculate purchase quantities for each ingredient. Eggs are purchased in boxes of 360 all other ingredients are purchased by the kg (1000g). Use a formula that will round the purchase quantity up to the nearest whole box or kg. Put a suitable title in cell A17 and add a thick red box border around this information.

(g)   Insert the quantities in column B as:

The Whirl   850

Splash   9

Butterbun   15

Chocco   24

(h)   Save the workbook.

TASK 6

The current selling prices for each cake are:

Cake	£
The Whirl	0.90
Splash	1.20
Butterbun	1.10
Chocco	1.50

(a)   Starting at Cell A23 on the budget spreadsheet, calculate whether the individual products are making a profit or a loss. You will need a column for cake, selling price, total cost, and profit.

(b)   Insert the selling price data for each cake from the list above in cells A24 to B28.

(c)   Use a VLOOKUP to look up the cost price from the 'Cost per Cake' worksheet in cells C24 to C28.

(d)   Use a formula in cells D24 to D28 to calculate profit.

(e)   Use conditional formatting to turn any cells in the profit column red where a product is loss making.

(f)   Put a thick box border in red around this table.

(g)   Show formulas and auto-fit to columns.

(h)   Set orientation to landscape.

(i)   Save your work.

TASK 7

(a)   Add a header to each worksheet, in the central box put in the name of each worksheet (as shown on each tab).

(b)   Add a footer to each worksheet, in the left hand box put your name and AAT registration number and in the right hand box put the date.

(c)   Save the workbook.

SCENARIO 3

CRAZY CARS

You work as a payroll assistant for a car sales company called Crazy Cars.

The sales team are paid a basic wage plus commission for the cars that they sell.

There are 7 members of sales staff, whose start dates at the company are as follows:

Name:	Start Date:
Ryan Lee	14/01/2009
Simon Mozley	28/03/2007
Jack Brown	08/02/2004
Stuart Gregson	01/09/2003
Linda Green	14/11/2003
Bev Jones	31/10/2007
Amrit Lad	16/08/2005

Basic wage

The basic wage is dependent on the number of full years each employee has worked for the business.

An employee's starting rate (for the first 12 months) is £160 per week.

The basic rate per week increases by 10% for each full year of employment up to a maximum of 5 years.

Commission earned

Each employee receives 5% of the profit they have earned from each car they have sold that week.

If a car is sold at a loss, then 5% of this loss is deducted from the employee's commission.

Any cars sold at a loss must be highlighted for the Finance Manager.

Weekly bonus

The member of staff who earns the most commission each week receives an extra £100 bonus.

If you are doing this exercise at your training provider you should save your work after each task to the folder designated for that purpose. If you are doing the exercise on your own computer we recommend that you create a folder to save your work in.

Required:

TASK 1

Set up a new spreadsheet for the scenario. Save this file as 'Crazy Cars'. The spreadsheet will need 4 worksheets.

Rename:

Worksheet 1   Employee Information

Worksheet 2   Basic Pay

Worksheet 3   Car Sales Information

Worksheet 4   Total Pay

Save your work.

TASK 2

On the 'Employee Information' worksheet:

(a)   Starting at column A, using suitable headings, input the employee names and their employment start dates.

(b)   Place the TODAY function in Cell B10. Add a suitable heading in Cell A10.

(c)   In column C calculate the number of days each employee has worked for Crazy Cars with reference to the TODAY function in Cell B10. Use absolute and relative referencing where appropriate. Change the format of these cells to general so the number of days is shown rather than the date.

(d)   In column D convert the number of days into years.

(e)   In column E use a formula to round the number of years down to the nearest year.

(f)   Show formulas and auto-fit column widths.

(g)   Save your work.

TASK 3

On the 'Basic Pay' worksheet:

(a)   Start your table in Cell A1, use column A for the number of years and column B for the basic weekly wage. Put suitable headings for both columns.

(b)   Using the information from the scenario on basic wages, calculate the weekly pay for an employee at the company based on 0 to 15 years of employment.

(c)   Format the basic wage to pounds and pence.

(d)   Add a border around each cell.

(e)   Show formulas and auto-fit column widths.

(f)   Save your work.

TASK 4

On the 'Car Sales Information' worksheet:

(a)   Import the data found in the 'Car Sales' text file into Sheet 1/cell $A$1. The text file can be found on MyKaplan in Practise, Revision Material, Revision Kit Additional Resources. The text file will need to be downloaded and saved before starting the task.

(b)   In column E create use a formula to calculate the profit made for each vehicle.

(c)   In column F calculate the amount of commission earned on each vehicle.

(d)   All monetary values should be formatted to currency (£) to 2 decimal places.

(e)   Use conditional formatting to identify any vehicles that have been sold at a loss. Have the cell turn red with black text.

(f)   Show formulas and auto-fit column widths.

(g)   Save your work.

TASK 5

Using the 'Car Sales Information' worksheet:

(a)   Create a pivot table in a new worksheet that shows the commission earned by each employee per make of car.

(b)   Format the values in the Pivot table as currency £ to 2 decimal places.

(c)   Name the Pivot Table worksheet as 'Pivot'.

(d)   Move the Pivot Table worksheet to the right of the Car Sales Information worksheet.

(e)   Save your work.

TASK 6

On the 'Total Pay' worksheet:

(a)   Type the following headings into the cells given:

(i)	Employee	A1
(ii)	Number of Years	B1
(iii)	Guaranteed Pay	C1
(iv)	Commission	D1
(v)	Bonus	E1
(vi)	Total pay for the week	F1

(b)   Show the following information:

   (i)   Column A, using Data Validation create a drop down list of all employees.

   (ii)   Column B, use a VLOOKUP from the 'Employee Information' tab to extract the number of years each employee has been employed.

   (iii) Column C, Use a VLOOKUP from the Basic Pay worksheet, to calculate the applicable basic weekly pay for each employee.

   (iv)   Column D, Use a VLOOKUP from the Pivot table worksheet, enter the Commission earned per employee.

   (v)   In cell D10 use a function to show the highest commission earned, add a suitable title in cell C10.

   (vi)   Column E, use an IF statement that refers to the maximum commission in cell D10 that will determine which employee has earned the most commission and therefore will earn the weekly bonus of £100.

   (vii) Column F, Using the Sum function – calculate the total pay for each employee for the week and the total wages the company are paying that week.

   (viii) Format all monetary amounts to pounds and pence.

   (ix)   Show formulas and auto-fit column widths.

TASK 7

The Finance Director wants to see how each sales person has contributed to the total commission earned.

(a)   Create a pie chart using the 'Total Pay' worksheet to show each employees commission as a proportion of the total commission.

(b)   Give the pie chart a suitable title and apply percentage labels to the chart.

(c)   Save this on a new worksheet called 'Pie Chart' and move the sheet to the right of the Total Pay worksheet.

(d)   Save your work.

TASK 8

(a)   Format the worksheets so that each worksheet fits on one page.

(b)   Save your work.

TASK 9

(a)   Add a header to each worksheet, in the central box put in the name of each worksheet (as shown on each tab).

(b)   Add a footer to each worksheet, in the left hand box put your name and AAT registration number and in the right hand box put the date.

(c)   Save the workbook.

SCENARIO 4

GOODTIME TRAVEL

Goodtime Travel is a firm of Travel Agents that specialises in long haul package holidays. They buy the flights and hotel rooms in bulk from the airlines and hotels. They are a reputable firm and get most of their custom from customers who have used their service before.

They have recently invested in a marketing campaign to try and encourage new customers to use their service. The Marketing Manager has said that the campaign will be viewed as a success if at least 40% of income each week is generated from new customers.

Repeat customers

Customers can receive discounts off their holidays. A discount will only be given if a customer has booked a previous holiday with Goodtime Travel. A discount is given of 2p per mile flown on the previous holiday.

This discount is then deducted from the price of the current holiday. However, the Finance Director is considering adapting the discount rates so that they are different for each destination. Details of the miles travelled for each destination are:

Miles (round trip) from Heathrow

Destination	Miles
Sydney	21,200
Fiji	20,218
Cape Town	12,010
Los Angeles	17,500
Hong Kong	12,104
Rio De Janeiro	18,004
Kuala Lumpar	13,104
Auckland	22,774
Beijing	10,140
Tokyo	11,874
Colombo (Sri Lanka)	10,816

Required:

TASK 1

Set up a new spreadsheet for the scenario. Save this file as 'Goodtime Travel'. The spreadsheet will need 3 worksheets.

Rename:

Worksheet 1	Discounts
Worksheet 2	Weekly sales
Worksheet 3	What If Analysis

TASK 2

On the 'Discounts' worksheet:

(a)   Starting at Cell A3, Input the all possible destinations, and their associated air-miles from the scenario data. Create suitable headings. Add a row for 'Not applicable' to the list of destinations, for customers who have not booked through Goodtime Travel before, with associated air-miles of 0.

(b)   In Cell E1 enter the discount rate given in the scenario and give it a suitable heading in D1.

(c)   In Column C create a formula to calculate the discount for a particular destination.

(d)   Format the discount column as currency (£) to 2 decimal places.

(e)   Show formulas, auto-fit column widths and save your work.

TASK 3

On the 'Weekly Sales' worksheet:

(a)   Copy and paste the week's sales information from the 'Weekly Bookings' word file into cell A1. The word file can be found on MyKaplan in Practise, Revision Material, Revision Kit Additional Resources. The word file will need to be downloaded and saved before starting the task.

(b)   Create a Discount column in column F. Use a VLOOKUP from the 'Discounts' worksheet to calculate any applicable discounts.

(c)   Format currency to 2 decimal places in £.

(d)   In the column G, use a formula to calculate the amount owing for each booking deducting any discounts for repeat customers.

(e)   Show formulas, auto-fit column widths, set the orientation to landscape and fit the data to one page.

(f)   Save the workbook.

TASK 4

(a)   Create a pivot table in a new worksheet to show how much revenue has been generated from new customers compared to existing customers for the different destinations.

(b)   Call this worksheet 'Pivot' and move it to the right of the 'Weekly sales' worksheet.

(c)   In cell K9 on the Pivot sheet create an expression to calculate the total % of income generated from new customers.

(d)   In cell K10 use an IF function – based on the outcome of task 4c – for the Marketing Director to determine whether the campaign was a success. 'Successful' should appear if more than 40% of the income is generated from new customers and 'Unsuccessful' if less than 40% of the income is generated from new customers. Format the outcome of the IF formula by making it bold, and enlarging the text to font size 16.

(e)   Show formulas, auto-fit column width and save your work.

TASK 5

The Finance Director is considering changing the discount on offer per mile for repeat customers. He wants the discounts amounts for the following destinations changed to:

Destination	New Discount	Currently
Sydney	£250.00	£424.00
Fiji	£300.00	£404.36

On the What If Analysis worksheet:

(a)   Copy all the Discount information from the discount worksheet into the What IF Analysis worksheet.

(b)   Using What If Analysis – Goal Seek, calculate what the revised discount rate per mile needs to be to reduce the discount offered for Sydney. Copy and 'paste–special values' the result to cell D20. Provide a suitable heading in A20. Reset the original discount rate per mile to 2p.

(c)   Using What If Analysis – Goal Seek, calculate what the revised discount rate per mile needs to be to reduce the discount offered for Fiji. Copy and 'paste–special values' the result to cell D22. Provide a suitable heading in A22. Reset the original discount rate per mile to 2p.

(d)   Show formulas, auto-fit column width and save your work.

TASK 6

(a)   Add a header to each worksheet, in the central box put in the name of each worksheet (as shown on each tab).

(b)   Add a footer to each worksheet, in the left hand box put your name and AAT registration number and in the right hand box put the date.

(c)   Save the workbook.

SCENARIO 5

STAR TICKETS

You work for Star Tickets, a small company selling tickets to music concerts.

Star Tickets buys tickets from concert venues to sell them on to customers. The face value of the tickets is £50, but Star Tickets receives discounts depending on which day the concert takes place. Star Tickets sales staff aim to sell each ticket for as much as possible; if they sell a ticket for more than its purchase price they receive a bonus. The discount percentages are:

Monday – Wednesday 25%

Thursday 10%

Friday–Sunday no discount is offered

Customers can pay in instalments, although management have said that at the end of each day the total outstanding balance owed by all customers cannot be greater than 10% of the total sales generated that day.

Management are also keen to identify any unpopular artists whose tickets are not making a profit for the company.

Star Tickets have asked you to help them create a spreadsheet to help manage their ticket sales. They have given you the details for today's sales:

Artist	Day of concert	Customer payment		Ticket seller
		Sales price	Amount paid	
Nancy Arbuckle	Saturday	£30	£10	Jane
Other Way	Tuesday	£60	£60	Mark
Down Stream	Wednesday	£90	£90	Mark
Upright Legs	Friday	£80	£80	Karen
Other Way	Tuesday	£30	£15	Jane
Nancy Arbuckle	Saturday	£45	£45	Mark
Down Stream	Friday	£34	£34	Jane

Required:

TASK 1

(a)   Create a new workbook and call it 'Star Tickets'.

(b)   Rename one worksheet 'Ticket Sales'; and another 'Data'. Delete any other worksheets.

TASK 2

The 'Data' worksheet will contain lists of artists, sellers and the various discounts to be used to calculate ticket prices on the Ticket Sales worksheet.

(a)   On the 'Data' worksheet:

- In column A list the names of the artists that Star tickets sell tickets for (Other Way, Upright Legs, Down Stream and Nancy Arbuckle)

- In column B list the days of week (Monday to Sunday)

- In column C list the ticket sellers' names (Karen, Mark and Jane).

(b)   On the 'Data' worksheet starting in cell E1, create a table of information to show the discounted prices that Star Tickets pay to the venues for the different days of the week. The table needs a column for the days of the week, Discount percentage, the original price, and the discounted price. Provide suitable headings. Use formulas to calculate the discounted price.

(c)   Auto-fit columns, set orientation to landscape and save the workbook.

TASK 3

(a)   Starting in Cell A1 on the 'Ticket Sales' worksheet insert the following column headings in bold:

Artist

Days of week

Ticket seller

Purchase price

Sales price

Amount paid

Amount outstanding

Profit/loss

Bonus payable?

(b)   Use 'Data Validation' to create drop down lists for Artist; Day of Week; Ticket Seller in columns A, B and C respectively. You will need to copy the 'data validation' down each column to row 8. Insert the information for today's sales from the table in the scenario. (Note: if you are using a version of Excel that is earlier than 2010 you will need to create a 'named range' for each drop down list before you can use Data Validation.)

(c)   In the 'Purchase Price' column, create a VLOOKUP that selects the correct discounted purchase price based on the day of the week.

(d)   Enter the data from the scenario for the 'Sales price' and 'Amount paid'.

(e)   In the 'Amount Outstanding' column create a formula that takes the 'Amount Paid' from the 'Sales Price'.

(f)   In the 'Profit/Loss' column create a formula that calculates the profit or a loss.

(g)   In the 'Bonus Payable?' column, create an 'IF' function to determine whether a bonus is due. If a bonus is due the function should return Yes if not then the function should return No.

(h)   Set all monetary amounts on each worksheet to currency £ and 2 decimal places.

(i)   Save your work.

TASK 4

(a)   On the 'Ticket Sales' worksheet use conditional formatting to fill cells red in the 'Profit/loss' column where a loss has been made.

(b)   Label Row 10 'Totals'. Create totals below the 'Sales Price' and the 'Amount Outstanding' column. Use single line border at the top of these cells and double line border at the bottom of the cells.

(c)   Indicate the cells that have been filled manually by highlighting them 'light blue'.

(d)   Any cells which are updated automatically need to be highlighted 'orange'.

(e)   In Cell G15 create a formula to determine how much of the sales are outstanding as a percentage of total sales made. Provide a suitable bold heading in cell F15 and right align the heading.

(f)   In cell H15 create an IF Function that determines whether the percentage would be acceptable to management. The function should return either 'OK' or 'Not Acceptable'.

(g)   Set orientation to landscape, show formulas, auto-fit column width, fit the data to one page and save your work.

TASK 5

(a)   Create a pivot table in a new worksheet to show how much profit each ticket seller has made, by Artist.

(b)   Using custom formatting hide the ticket sellers' names in the pivot table.

(c)   Rename the worksheet 'Pivot' and move it to the right of the 'Ticket Sales' worksheet.

(d)   Use conditional formatting to highlight the cells yellow in the pivot table where a loss has been made.

(e)   Save your work.

TASK 6

(a)   Add a header to each worksheet, in the central box put in the name of each worksheet (as shown on each tab).

(b)   Add a footer to each worksheet, in the left hand box put your name and AAT registration number and in the right hand box put the date.

(c)   Save the workbook.

Section 3

ANSWERS TO EXAM – PART I PRACTICE TASKS

TASK 1.1

1 DILIGENCE

	Yes	No
Continue with forging a relationship with the client		✓
Inform the client that without knowing the correct address the client/accountant relationship cannot be forged	✓	
Consider reporting the conversation to NCA.	✓	

To comply with customer due diligence (part of money laundering regulations), the best course of action for Connor to take would be to inform the client that without knowing the correct address the client/accountant relationship cannot be forged.

The reluctance to disclose an address raises concerns over possible money laundering, so Connor must consider reporting the conversation to NCA.

2 JESS

(a)

	Yes	No
Integrity		
Confidentiality		
Professional competence and due care	✓	
Professional behaviour		
Objectivity		

3   REFERENCE

(a)   The ethical principles involved here are as follows:

- **Integrity** – Steve must be straightforward and honest in all professional and business relationships. Integrity also implies fair dealing and truthfulness and there is a danger that the reference is not a fair or true representation of the facts as he sees them.

- **Objectivity** – the large fee should not be allowed to colour Steve's judgement. This presents a self-interest threat.

  It could also be argued that, because Kept Ltd is Steve's oldest client, then there is also a familiarity threat to objectivity.

- **Professional behaviour** – writing a reference that Steve suspects to be false could bring discredit to himself and the profession.

(b)   Steve is potentially guilty of 'fraud by false representation' under the Fraud Act 2006. This is where a person makes 'any representation as to fact or law ... express or implied' which they know to be untrue or misleading.

There is also the possibility that the large fee could be interpreted as a bribe under the Bribery Act 2010 and Steve could be found guilty of passive bribery (receiving a bribe) under the Act.

(c)   It is acceptable practice for Steve to include a disclaimer of liability and it certainly does no harm to include one. However, disclaimers can be challenged in court so may not afford Steve any protection.

If he has serious doubts over whether or not Kept Ltd will be able to pay the rent, then he shouldn't write the reference.

4   CYCLE

(a)   Mthbe needs to keep up-to-date in the following areas (only TWO needed):

- tax legislation/compliance

- money laundering regulations

- accounting/reporting standards

- regulation of accounting.

The reasons for this are as follows:

- They are important areas because clients are businesses, which must comply with requirement for accurate accounts preparation and tax returns.

- Mthbe needs to ensure he is technically competent to undertake the work (fundamental principle of professional competence and due care).

- Mthbe needs to protect himself re money laundering.

(b)   The AAT CPD policy asks Mthbe to update his skills twice a year.

(c)   The AAT's CPD cycle has four stages – assess, plan, action and evaluation.

5 SARAH

(a) Sarah should obtain authority from the client to give the financial information.

(b) It is not possible to give an assurance regarding the client ability to pay the rent.

6 KUTCHINS

Gemma is allowed to use general knowledge and experience from a previous employer but NOT specific information from that employer that is covered by the duty of confidentiality.

This means that general accountancy, audit and management skills and knowledge can all be used but not specific information concerning Kirk Ltd.

7 BEVIS

Matter 1

Bevis should NOT tell the Managing Director anything that would be considered 'private information' as this would be a breach of confidentiality.

Matter 2

Bevis should tell the customer that he has been unable to gain the information.

Pretending to be a customer lacks integrity and would not be acting professionally.

8 NIGHT OUT

(a)

Integrity	
Confidentiality	
Professional competence and due care	
Professional behaviour	✓
Objectivity	

(b) Bella should suggest to the Finance Director that he should replace the sign, and possibly discuss the matter with the Managing Director.

9 DILEMMA

(a)

Integrity	
Confidentiality	✓
Professional competence and due care	
Professional behaviour	
Objectivity	

(b)

From an ethical point of view you should tell your friend about the redundancies on the grounds it could save her unnecessary financial problems and distress.	
You should not tell your friend about the redundancies.	✓

You should not tell your friend about the redundancies as to do so would breach confidentiality.

10 JUSTIN

(a) This situation presents a self-interest threat.

(b) The best course of action is to remove Justin from this assurance engagement.

11 JULIE

(a) This situation presents a self-interest threat.

(b) Two safeguards the assurance firm should have in place are:

- A policy requiring the immediate disclosure of such an offer of employment

- A policy requiring Julie to be removed from the assurance engagement.

12 NO DEFENCE

(a) The Bribery Act 2010 creates four offences:

1   bribing a person to induce or reward them to perform a relevant function improperly

2   requesting, accepting or receiving a bribe as a reward for performing a relevant function improperly

3   using a bribe to influence a foreign official to gain a business advantage

4   a new form of corporate liability for failing to prevent bribery on behalf of a commercial organisation.

(b) For a commercial organisation, it is a defence to have in place 'adequate procedures' to prevent bribery.

This may include implementing anti-bribery procedures.

It is important that firms consider what procedures are 'adequate' for their firm given the risks they face and the way they run their business. The procedures should be proportionate to the risk posed.

For some firms there will be no need to put bribery prevention procedures in place as there is no risk of bribery on their behalf. Other firms may need to put measures in place in key areas, such as gifts and hospitality, as this is the area where they have identified a risk.

Corporate ignorance of individual wrongdoing will provide no protection against prosecution.

(c)   Certainly the excessive nature of the hospitality would mean that it would be viewed as an attempt to bribe the MP concerned.

While M plc could argue that they are not guilty of 1, 2 and 3 above, they are likely to be found guilty under offence 4.

Even though Mr Igbinadola was an agent and not an employee and even though the Board claim ignorance, the company could still be found guilty of failing to prevent bribery.

The only possible defence would be to demonstrate that they had adequate procedures in place to prevent bribery, but in this case it looks difficult to prove this.

13   L PLC

Arguing that an activity complies with 'local law' or 'customs and practices' is no defence under the Bribery Act.

If L plc goes ahead with the request, then two offences under the Act will have been committed:

1   Using a bribe (the donations) to influence a foreign official to gain a business advantage.

2   Failing to prevent bribery on behalf of a commercial organisation.

L plc should thus refuse the request for 'donations'.

14   IN-HOUSE CODE

The code is a voluntary one prepared by John Grooms Ltd for its own use.

It cannot insist on suppliers adopting it.

The code cannot be statutory since that would be created under legislation/regulation/ case law and used by many companies.

15   NEW CODE

1   *All products should be purchased from local farms and suppliers where appropriate.*

This would have a positive impact from a sustainability perspective as it would reduce distribution miles and the associated impact on fossil fuels and pollution.

The main reservation is the wording 'where appropriate' as there is no indication as to what 'appropriate' means – for example, Cosby could buy cheaper goods from overseas suppliers and argue that the low cost made it 'appropriate'.

2   *All packing materials should be obtained from renewable sources where feasible.*

This would also have a positive impact from a sustainability perspective as it would reduce deforestation to provide cardboard and paper packaging.

The main reservation is the wording 'where feasible' as there is no indication as to what 'feasible' means – for example, Cosby could buy cheaper goods with plastic packaging and argue that the low cost made it 'feasible'.

3   *All suppliers to be paid on time.*

This should mean that suppliers are treated fairly. However, there is no indication that suppliers have any say in what constitutes 'on time'.

4   *All suppliers to be paid fair prices as determined by the Purchasing Manager.*

This should also mean that suppliers are treated fairly.

However, there is no indication that suppliers have any say in what constitutes 'fair prices' – the price needs to be seen to be reasonable and fair by both parties.

16 PROCEDURE

(a)   Ye Lin must cooperative fully with the investigation.

(b)   If Ye Lin fails to cooperate as an AAT member she could be found guilty of **misconduct**.

(c)   The AAT could apply the following disciplinary actions:

- Be expelled from the Association

- Have her membership of the Association suspended

- Have her practicing licence withdrawn.

17 CHRIS

(a)   This situation represents a threat to the fundamental principles of

- Objectivity – because it is difficult to act without a perception of bias when the two clients' interests are in such conflict because they both want a price and terms beneficial to themselves; and

- Confidentiality – because he has confidential information in respect of each client.

(b)   Chris should:

- consider relevant facts/ethical issues involved/his fundamental principles/any established procedures in HJK and Co

- establish alternative courses of action, establish which is most consistent with the fundamental principles and establish the consequences of each

- seek advice about the matter within HJK and Co, and document the substance of the issue and discussions.

(c)   In acting for one of the clients Chris should consider instituting appropriate safeguards so that his familiarity with the other client does not affect his professional judgement/objectivity, and so that he does not breach confidentiality re the other party.

18 SIMON

(a)   This situation represents a self-interest threat.

(b)   Simon's best course of action is to sell the shares or, failing that, to ask to be removed from the audit engagement.

19   LAST

    (a)   This situation displays a breach of Confidentiality.

    (b)   Jason's friend, Brian, should talk to the director concerned and explained that to act in the way suggested would be unethical.

           (**Note:** you could have answered that he should get advice without breaching confidentiality, say by ringing the AAT ethics helpline.)

    (c)   Brian should resign and state the reason for the resignation. Then report the situation to the external regulators.

20   SAFE AND SOUND

Matter A

The ethical threat is basically one of self-interest.

The director is using price sensitive information to ensure that a loss is prevented by selling shares now rather than after the announcement of poor results for the company.

One ethical safeguard would be a professional code of conduct that requires directors to carry out their duties with integrity and therefore in the best interests of the shareholders. The director would recognise that selling the shares would start the share price falling already and this would not benefit the shareholders.

As a code it may not be effective – the director could argue that selling shares prior to the results was designed to warn shareholders of the imminent fall in share price and was, therefore, in their best interests.

An alternative course of action is to ban trading in shares a given number of weeks prior to the announcement of company results (as happens in the USA where directors are not allowed to sell shares during 'blackout periods'). This would be effective as share sales can be identified and the directors could incur a penalty for breach of legislation.

Matter B

The ethical threat appears to be a lack of independence and self-interest regarding the setting of remuneration for these directors.

Not only do they have common directorships, but they are also good friends. They could easily vote for higher than normal remuneration packages for each other on the remuneration committees knowing that the other director will reciprocate on the other remuneration committee.

In corporate governance terms, one ethical safeguard is to ban these cross-directorships.

The ban would be enforceable as the directors of companies must be stated in annual accounts, hence it would be easy to identify cross-directorships. The ban would also be effective as the conflict of interest would be removed.

In professional terms, the directors clearly have a conflict of interest. While their professional code of ethics may mention this precisely as an ethical threat, Graham and Mike should follow the spirit of the code and resign their non-executive directorships.

This again would remove the threat.

Matter C

There is a clear ethical threat to the directors of Company Z.

They appear to be being bribed so that they do not query the management style of the chairman. The threat is that the directors will simply accept the benefits given to them rather than try to run Company Z in the interests of the shareholders. It is clearly easy to accept that option.

Ethical safeguards are difficult to identify and their application depends primarily on the desire of the directors to take ethical actions. In overall terms, the chairman does not appear to be directly breaching ethical or governance codes. The main safeguard is therefore for the directors not to accept appointment as director to Company Z or resign from the board if already a director.

The director could attempt to get the matter discussed at board level, although it is unlikely the chairman would allow this. Taking any other action is in effect 'whistle blowing' on all the directors and has the negative impact that the director would also have to admit to receiving 'benefits' from the company.

21 FREE HOLIDAYS

The Bribery Act 2010 creates four offences:

1   bribing a person to induce or reward them to perform a relevant function improperly

2   requesting, accepting or receiving a bribe as a reward for performing a relevant function improperly

3   using a bribe to influence a foreign official to gain a business advantage

4   a new form of corporate liability for failing to prevent bribery on behalf of a commercial organisation.

Leigh Davis is guilty of bribery (offence 1 above) under the Act as he is bribing Sarah by offering her free holidays in return for her performing her function as an audit manager improperly.

Sarah is guilty of receiving a bribe (offence 2 above) from Leigh Davis.

B & Sons LLP could also be guilty of bribery of the Act for failing to prevent bribery (offence 4 above) unless they can show that they had in place 'adequate procedures'.

Both Leigh and Sarah could receive a maximum jail sentence of up to ten years.

If B & Sons LLP is found guilty they could be liable for an unlimited fine.

22 KEN

(a)   Money laundering is the process by which the proceeds of crime, either money or other property, are converted into assets, which appear to have a legitimate rather than an illegal origin. The aim of the process is to disguise the source of the property, in order to allow the holder to enjoy it free from suspicion as to its source.

The Proceeds of Crime Act 2002 (POCA) seeks to control money laundering by creating three categories of criminal offences in relation to the activity.

Laundering

Under the POCA, the three money laundering offences are

- s327 – Concealing, disguising, converting, transferring or removing criminal property.

- s328 – Taking part in an arrangement to facilitate the acquisition, use or control of criminal property.

- s329 – Acquiring, using or possessing criminal property.

These offences are punishable on conviction by a maximum of 14 years' imprisonment and/or a fine.

Failure to report

The second category of offence relates to failing to report a knowledge or suspicion of money laundering.

It is an offence for a person who knows or suspects that another person is engaged in money laundering not to report the fact to the appropriate authority.

However, the offence only relates to individuals, such as accountants, who are acting in the course of business in the regulated sector.

The offences set out in these sections are punishable on conviction by a maximum of five years' imprisonment and/or a fine.

Tipping off

The third category of offence relates to tipping off. It is an offence to make a disclosure which is likely to prejudice any investigation under the Act.

The offences set out in these sections are punishable on conviction by a maximum of five years' imprisonment and/or a fine.

(b)   Ken would therefore be guilty of the primary offence of money laundering as explained in the section above.

Los is also guilty of an offence in relation to the Proceeds of Crime Act as he is clearly assisting Ken in his money laundering procedure. He is actively concealing and disguising criminal property, and his arrangement with Ken facilitates the retention of criminal property.

Mel is equally guilty under the same provisions as Los, in that he is actively engaged in the money laundering process, by producing false accounts.

23   MLRO

(a)   Jeff has just committed the offence of tipping off.

(b)   The maximum sentence is 5 years.

(c)   In the absence of an MLRO, Jeff should have approached NCA with his concerns.

(d)   De minimus means no minimum limit.

24 ADAM

Matter 1

Adam is obliged to report this refusal to disclose and the information surrounding it to the firm's Money Laundering Reporting Officer (MLRO).

Matter 2

This scenario also gives grounds for suspicion of money laundering. Why doesn't the client, H Ltd, simply want LOFT to repay them and then it up to them whether they want to pay anything to Q Ltd? Is it to make funds difficult to trace, so 'dirty cash' becomes a nice clean cheque from a reputable accounting firm?

Any overpayment by a customer should be thoroughly investigated by a senior member of finance function staff and only repaid to the customer once it has been established that it is right/legal to do so.

Similarly the request to pay a third party should be scrutinised before any payment is agreed to. Without further information the transaction does not make commercial sense.

Unless investigations satisfy any concerns raised, then LOFT should refuse the payment and the MRLO should fill in a Suspicious Activity Report (SAR) to be sent to the NCA (previously known as SOCA).

25 DONNA

	True	False
Funds retained after discovery of a tax error amount to money laundering by Stoppard plc	✓	
Donna should report the matter to the National Crime Agency (NCA)	✓	
Donna needs to make an authorised disclosure to the National Crime Agency NCA	✓	

Funds dishonestly retained after discovery of a tax error become criminal property so their retention amounts to money laundering by Stoppard plc.

As she is now aware of the error, Donna should report to the National Crime Agency (NCA) that she suspects Stoppard plc of money laundering because it has refused to notify the matter to HMRC. She will be protected from a claim for breach of confidentiality when making this report.

Knowing she may have been involved in money laundering, Donna needs to make an authorised disclosure to NCA which may help protect her from a charge that she herself, in making the error, was engaged in money laundering.

TASK 1.2

26 EMMA

VAT payable for the period ended 31 March 2017

	£	£
Output VAT		
Standard rated sales (£450,000 × 20%)		90,000
Discounts taken (£225,000 × 4% × 20%)		(1,800)
Zero rated sales		0
		————
		88,200
Input VAT		
Inventory (£180,000 × 20%)	36,000	
Electricity (£40,000 × 1/6)	6,667	
Car expenses (£15,000 × 1/6)	2,500	
Irrecoverable debts (£1,200 × 20%)	240	
	————	(45,407)
		————
VAT payable		42,793
		————

Tutorial note

Where a prompt payment discount is offered output VAT is charged on the actual amount received, i.e. for the invoices which were settled within 30 days output VAT is due on the value of the sale less the 4% discount. However, the supplier will not know, when the invoice is raised, whether the customer will qualify for the discount by paying promptly. The supplier must therefore charge VAT on the invoice on the full price.

If the discount is taken the supplier must then make an adjustment so that output tax is only accounted for on the amount received.

Irrecoverable debt relief is only available on debts over six months old, so relief cannot yet be claimed on the debt due on 13 October 2016.

To find the amount of VAT on a VAT inclusive figure you multiply by 20/120. This fraction is usually simplified to 1/6.

27   MONTY FINCH

(a)   VAT penalties

Late notification penalties are a percentage of the net VAT due from the date Monty should have been registered until the date when notification is made:

*   The percentage is based on the standard penalty regime for late notification and incorrect returns which applies across all taxes.

*   The penalty can range from 0% to 100% of the unpaid tax depending on the taxpayer's behaviour and whether disclosure is prompted or unprompted.

Tutorial note

You cannot calculate the amount of penalty as it is a % of the VAT due.

(b)   Blocked VAT

VAT is blocked and therefore cannot be recovered on the following items:

*   Motor cars not used 100% for business purposes

*   Business entertainment except for staff and overseas customers.

Tutorial note

Input VAT can be recovered on entertainment of employees and overseas customers.

28   BOB HAWKES

(a)   Tax points

The basic tax point is usually the earliest of the following dates:

The date of delivery	16 July 2016
The date of the invoice	20 July 2016
The date of payment	14 May 2016 (deposit) and 31 August 2016 (balance).

Therefore the tax point for the deposit will be 14 May 2016.

However, as regards the balance, the invoice date of 20 July 2016 will apply as the invoice was issued within 14 days of the delivery date.

Tutorial note

The basic tax point is the date of delivery of goods or the date of performance of services.

However, if goods or services are paid for in advance or a tax invoice is issued in advance, the date of payment or the invoice date becomes the tax point date. If a part payment such as a deposit is paid in advance then there will be two tax points, one for the deposit and one for the balance of the supply.

Where goods are not paid for or invoiced in advance, a later tax point can arise if a tax invoice is raised within 14 days after the basic tax point. This is referred to as the '14 day rule'.

(b)   If goods are supplied on a sale or return basis, the tax point is the earlier of the date of adoption by the customer or 12 months after the dispatch of the goods to the customer.

(c)   For continuous supplies of services, the tax point is the earlier of the receipt of payment or the date of the VAT invoice.

29   YEE-LING

(a)   Tax point (time of supply) for VAT

The basic tax point is the date the goods are dispatched or otherwise made available to the customer.

However the basic tax point is overridden in the following circumstances:

(i)   If an invoice is issued or payment is received before the goods are dispatched. In this case the earliest of these dates replaces the dispatch date.

(ii)   If a tax point has not already arisen under (i) above and an invoice is issued within 14 days after the goods have been dispatched. The invoice date will then replace the dispatch date.

(b)   Tax point for the transaction

The tax points for the transaction are therefore:

For the deposit of £400:   28 May 2016 (cash receipt)

For the balance of £2,600:   2 July 2016 (14 day rule)

(c)   Importance of determining the correct tax point

Any two of the following are acceptable:

- To calculate the turnover for initial registration.

- To include the sale in the correct VAT return.

- To identify the correct rate of VAT (if there is a change).

- To identify the correct category of VAT (zero rate, reduced rate, standard rate or exempt – if there is a change).

Tutorial note

The basic tax point is the date of delivery of goods or the date of performance of services.

However, if goods or services are paid for in advance or a tax invoice is issued in advance, the date of payment or the invoice date becomes the tax point date. If a part payment such as a deposit is paid in advance then there will be two tax points, one for the deposit and one for the balance of the supply.

Where goods are not paid for or invoiced in advance, a later tax point can arise if a tax invoice is raised within 14 days after the basic tax point. This is referred to as the '14 day rule'.

30   MARTHA

(a)   Martha – Value added tax (VAT) registration

The VAT registration threshold is £83,000. Martha's taxable turnover will exceed this at the end of March 2017 (£13,900 × 6 months = £83,400). Martha must therefore notify HMRC within 30 days (i.e. 30 April 2017).

Martha will be registered from the first day of the second month following the month in which the £83,000 was exceeded (i.e. 1 May 2017) (or an earlier date, if requested).

Tutorial note

The historic registration test is based on achieving £83,000 of taxable turnover in the last 12 months or since starting in business if this is less than 12 months. Taxable turnover excludes exempt supplies but includes zero rated supplies.

(b) **Recovery of pre-registration VAT**

Input VAT can be recovered on goods purchased prior to registration provided the goods were acquired for business purposes, and were not sold or consumed prior to registration. The goods must also have been acquired in the four years prior to registration. Input VAT can be recovered on services supplied prior to registration provided the services were supplied for business purposes within the six months prior to registration.

Tutorial note

Goods can be non-current assets or inventory. For example, if a trader buys a computer for their business but registers for VAT four months later, they can reclaim the input VAT on the computer on the first VAT return provided they still use it for business at the time of registration.

31 SEA, SAND AND SURF LTD

VAT – quarter ended 31 December 2016	£	£
Output VAT:		
Standard rated sales (£120,000 × 20%)		24,000
Input VAT:		
Purchases of goods for resale (£58,000 × 20%)	11,600	
Plant and machinery (£20,000 × 20%)	4,000	
Electricity (£3,525 × 1/6)	588	
Accountant's fees (£1,410 ×1/6)	235	
Irrecoverable debts (£600 × 20%)	120	
	———	(16,543)
		———
VAT payable		7,457
		———

Zero rated supplies – VAT at 0%, so no output tax due.

Wages – outside the scope of VAT

Insurance – exempt supply

Irrecoverable debt due in August 2016 – not more than six months old.

Tutorial note

Irrecoverable debt relief is only available on debts over 6 months old so relief cannot yet be claimed on the debt due in August 2016.

To find the amount of VAT in a VAT inclusive figure you multiply by 20/120. This fraction is usually simplified to 1/6.

32   ATHLETIC LTD

(a)   **Athletic Ltd – Notification of VAT registration**

		£
1 December 2016 – 28 February 2017		22,000
1 March 2017 – 31 May 2017		24,000
June 2017	(£57,000 × 1/3)	19,000
July 2017	(£57,000 × 1/3)	19,000
		84,000

The £83,000 threshold is exceeded at the end of July 2017.

Athletic Ltd must notify HMRC by 30 August 2017 (i.e. within 30 days of the end of July 2017).

(b)   **Compulsory registration date**

Athletic Ltd will be registered on 1 September 2017 (i.e. the first day of the second month following the month the threshold is exceeded).

(c)   **VAT periods**

The normal length of a VAT return is 3 calendar months.

The VAT return must be submitted online together with any VAT due within one month and 7 days of the end of the VAT period.

(d)   **Advantages and disadvantages of voluntary registration**

Advantages   Registration creates an impression of substantial business activity.

Input tax may be reclaimed.

Disadvantages   VAT records will have to be kept and compliance requirements met.

Customers will have 20% added to their bills. VAT registered customers will be able to reclaim the VAT suffered, however, non-VAT registered customers will not.

Tutorial note

The historic registration test is based on achieving £83,000 of taxable turnover in the last 12 months or since starting in business if this is less than 12 months. Taxable turnover excludes exempt supplies but includes zero rated supplies.

Voluntary registration is possible if a business is making or intending to make taxable supplies.

---

33   EMAIL

E mail to Financial Accountant

To:	Financial Accountant
From:	Junior accountant
Date:	16 July 2017
Subject:	**VAT return**

Please be advised that I have just completed the VAT return for the quarter ended 30 June 2017. The amount of VAT payable is £11,657.42.

This should be paid electronically with the submission of the VAT return by 7 August 2017.

The amount of VAT due will need to be included in the company cash flow forecasts to ensure that there will be sufficient funds available in the company bank account on the due date.

Kind regards

Junior accountant

34   VECTOR LTD

VAT return – Quarter ended 31 March 2017

	£	£
Output VAT		
Sales – standard rated (£128,000 × 20%)		25,600
Sales – zero rated		0
Deposit (£4,500 × 1/6)		750
		———
		26,350
Input VAT		
Expenses (£74,800 – £4,200) × 20%	14,120	
Irrecoverable debts (£800 + £800)	1,600	
Plant (£16,500 × 1/6)	2,750	
	———	(18,470)
		———
VAT payable		7,880
		———

No VAT input tax reclaimable on the car.

Tutorial note

1   Irrecoverable debt relief is only available on debts which were due for payment six months prior to 31 March 2017 (the end of the VAT period) so relief cannot yet be claimed on the debt due in October 2016.

2   The basic tax point is the date of delivery of goods or the date of performance of services. However, if goods or services are paid for in advance or a tax invoice is issued in advance, the date of payment or the invoice date becomes the tax point date. If a part payment such as a deposit is paid in advance then there will be two tax points, one for the deposit and one for the balance of the supply.

3   To find the amount of VAT in a VAT inclusive figure you multiply by 20/120. This fraction is usually simplified to 1/6.

35   DYNAMO LTD

Compulsory registration

Dynamo Ltd will become liable to register for VAT when its taxable supplies during any 12 month period exceed £83,000.

Dynamo Ltd will exceed the threshold in November 2017 as shown below:

12 months to the end of:	October 2017	November 2017
	£	£
November 2016	4,100	–
December 2016	4,000	4,000
January 2017	4,400	4,400
February 2017	5,000	5,000
March 2017	4,900	4,900
April 2017	5,600	5,600
May 2017	6,500	6,500
June 2017	6,600	6,600
July 2017	6,800	6,800
August 2017	7,500	7,500
September 2017	10,100	10,100
October 2017	10,200	10,200
November 2017	–	11,800
	———	———
	75,700	83,400
	———	———
	< £83,000	> £83,000
Need to register?	No	Yes

Dynamo Ltd will have to notify HM Revenue and Customs by 30 December 2017, being 30 days after the end of the month when the registration threshold was exceeded.

The company will be registered from 1 January 2018 or from an agreed earlier date and must charge VAT on taxable supplies from this date.

Tutorial note

The historic registration test is based on achieving £83,000 of taxable turnover in the last 12 months or since starting in business if this is less than 12 months. Taxable turnover excludes exempt supplies but includes zero rated supplies.

In a question like this you should add up the sales for the first 12 months of trading. If they exceed the registration threshold then take off one month at a time until you reach the month in which the threshold is first exceeded.

If the total for the first 12 months is less than the registration threshold then add on the next month's sales, but deduct the sales for the first month of trading so you are only looking back at 12 months in total. Repeat this until you find the month in which the total first exceeds the threshold.

36 BATTERY LTD

(a) VAT invoice

The following additional information is required:

1   Battery Ltd's VAT registration number.

2   The tax point.

3   The rate of VAT for each supply.

4   The VAT exclusive amount for each supply.

5   The total VAT exclusive amount.

6   The amount of VAT payable.

(b) Future turnover test for registration

If taxable supplies in the next 30 days in isolation are expected to exceed the annual registration threshold, HMRC should be notified within 30 days of that date. Registration is effective from the beginning of the 30-day period.

37   CONFUSED LTD

(a)   Registration and VAT due

Standard rated supplies

Confused Ltd will be required to register for VAT as it is making taxable supplies in excess of the registration threshold of £83,000.

Output VAT of £16,800 (£84,000 × 20%) per month will be due, and input VAT of £1,667 (£10,000 × 1/6) per month will be recoverable.

Tutorial note

To find the amount of VAT in a VAT inclusive figure you multiply by 20/120. This fraction is usually simplified to 1/6.

Zero rated supplies

Confused Ltd is permitted to register for VAT, but is not required to register, as it is only making zero rated supplies.

Output VAT will not be due, but input VAT of £1,667 per month will be recoverable, assuming Confused Ltd registers for VAT.

Exempt supplies

Confused Ltd will not be required or permitted to register for VAT as it will not be making taxable supplies.

Output VAT will not be due and no input VAT will be recoverable.

(b)   Voluntary disclosure of errors

If the net errors total less than the higher of £10,000 or 1% turnover (capped at £50,000), they can be voluntarily disclosed by entering them on the next VAT return.

If the net errors exceed this figure, they cannot be entered on the next return. Instead, disclosure must be made separately to HM Revenue and Customs.

Tutorial note

When a trader discovers a VAT error they must inform HMRC. If the net error is less than a certain limit and is not deliberate, it can be included on the next VAT return.

If not, it must be disclosed separately on a form or in a letter.

The limit operates as follows:

−   *Net errors up to £10,000 can always be included on the next VAT return.*

−   *Net errors above £50,000 must always be separately disclosed.*

−   *Errors between these limits can be included on the next VAT return if they are no more than 1% of turnover.*

38 VAT ERRORS

	Net error	Turnover	Treatment
	£	£	
1	24,567	2,000,000	The error is between £10,000 and £50,000 so it can be included on the next VAT return if it is ≤ 1% of turnover.
			1% of £2,000,000 is only £20,000 so the error must be separately disclosed.
2	4,568	85,400	This error can automatically be corrected on the next VAT return as it is less than £10,000.
3	35,980	4,567,090	The error is between £10,000 and £50,000 so it can be included on the next VAT return if it is ≤ 1% of turnover.
			1% of £4,567,090 is £45,671 so this error can be included on the next VAT return.
4	51,600	10,000,000	This error must be separately disclosed as it exceeds £50,000.

Tutorial note

When a trader discovers a VAT error they must inform HMRC. If the net error is less than a certain limit and is not deliberate, it can be included on the next VAT return. If not, it must be disclosed separately on a form or in a letter.

The limit operates as follows:

– *Net errors up to £10,000 can always be included on the next VAT return.*

– *Net errors above £50,000 must always be separately disclosed.*

– *Errors between these limits can be included on the next VAT return if they are no more than 1% of turnover.*

39 ASTUTE LTD

Annual accounting scheme

Astute Ltd can apply to use the annual accounting scheme if its expected taxable turnover for the next 12 months does not exceed £1,350,000 exclusive of VAT. The company must also be up to date with its VAT returns.

The company will only have to submit one VAT return each year. This should mean that default surcharges are avoided in respect of the late submission of VAT returns.

The company will be required to make payments on account based on the previous year's VAT liability. This will improve both budgeting and possibly cash flow if the business is expanding.

Tutorial note

The annual accounting scheme allows businesses to submit one VAT return each year. This is due two months after the year end.

VAT payments on account have to be made throughout the year. VAT is not just paid once a year with the return. These payments on account are based on last year's VAT liability.

40   BRIGHT LTD

Flat rate scheme

Bright Ltd can use the flat rate scheme if its expected taxable turnover for the next 12 months does not exceed £150,000.

The main advantage of the scheme is the simplified VAT administration as there is no need to keep detailed records of input VAT suffered.

In addition, in this question, as Bright Ltd's customers are not VAT registered there will be no need to issue VAT invoices which gives an added administrative advantage.

Tax savings can also be made, although this is not usually the primary reason for joining the scheme.

Using the normal basis of calculating the VAT liability, Bright Ltd will have to pay annual VAT of £10,833 (£75,000 – £10,000 = £65,000 × 1/6).

Whereas if Bright Ltd uses the flat rate scheme, it will pay VAT of £9,000 (£75,000 × 12%), which is the flat rate percentage applied to the VAT inclusive total turnover of the business.

An annual saving of £1,833 (£10,833 – £9,000) will be achieved under the flat rate scheme.

Note that under the flat rate scheme Bright Ltd does not recover any input tax on specific purchases and details of VAT on each purchase and expense does not need to be calculated.

Tutorial note

The flat rate percentage used by a business is fixed by reference to the average outputs less inputs for a typical business in that particular trade sector.

A business can join the flat rate scheme provided their taxable turnover (excluding VAT) is less than £150,000. They have to leave the scheme when their total turnover exceeds £230,000 (including VAT and exempt supplies.)

The VAT calculation is based on VAT inclusive TOTAL turnover, not just taxable turnover.

It is possible for a business to pay less VAT under the flat rate scheme than under the normal accounting scheme.

41   CLEVER LTD

Cash accounting scheme

Clever Ltd can use the cash accounting scheme if its expected taxable turnover for the next 12 months does not exceed £1,350,000 exclusive of VAT. The company must also be up to date with its VAT returns and VAT payments.

The scheme is advantageous as output VAT will be accounted for three months later than at present as the tax point will be the date that payment is received from customers. The recovery of input VAT on expenses will not be affected as these are paid in cash.

The scheme will also provide automatic irrecoverable debt relief should a customer default on the payment of a debt as output tax is not payable until the customer pays the debt.

Tutorial note

The cash accounting scheme allows businesses to pay over output tax when customers pay and reclaim input tax when suppliers are paid. Output and input VAT totals are taken from the cash book.

With the cash accounting scheme, the tax point date is the date the payment is received.

42   CITY MERCHANDISE LTD

VAT – quarter ended 31 March 2017

	£	£
Standard rated sales (£110,000 × 20%) (Note 1)		22,000
Discount adjustment (£55,000 × 5% × 20%) (Note 1)		(550)
Standard rated purchases (£60,000 × 20%)	12,000	
Electricity (£4,000 × 1/6) (Note 2)	667	
Repairs (£2,500 × 1/6)	417	
Entertaining UK customers (blocked) (Note 3)	0	
Entertaining overseas customers (£900 × 1/6)	150	
Car (£12,600 × 1/6)	2,100	
	———	(15,334)
VAT payable		6,116

Wages are outside the scope of VAT and no output VAT is due on zero rated supplies.

The VAT must be paid electronically by 7 May 2017 (i.e. one month and seven days after the quarter end).

Tutorial note

1   *Where a prompt payment discount is offered output VAT is charged on the actual amount received, i.e. for the invoices which were settled within 30 days output VAT is due on the value of the sale less the 5% discount. However, the supplier will not know, when the invoice is raised, whether the customer will qualify for the discount by paying promptly. The supplier must therefore charge VAT on the invoice on the full price. If the discount is taken the supplier must then make an adjustment so that output tax is only accounted for on the amount received.*

2   *To find the amount of VAT in a VAT inclusive figure you multiply by 20/120. This fraction is usually simplified to 1/6.*

3   *VAT is recoverable on entertaining overseas customers but not UK customers.*

43   DEFINITIONS

(a)   A taxable person is someone who is or is required to be registered for VAT.

A taxable person can be a company, partnership or individual.

(b)   In order for a supply to be a taxable supply it must be made:

(i)   by a taxable person

(ii)   for a consideration

(iii)   in the UK

(iv)   in the course or furtherance of a business.

44   BROADHURST

Box 1	£34,849
Box 4	(£22,348)
Box 5	£12,501
Box 6	£175,560
Box 7	£123,981

Workings:

(W1) Output VAT

	£
Sales (£175,560 × 20%)	35,112
Discounts (£131,670 × 1% × 20%)	(263)
	─────
	34,849
	─────

(W2) Input VAT

	£
Purchases (£113,670 × 20%)	22,734
Purchase returns (£5,249 × 20%)	(1,050)
Entertaining overseas customers (£1,560 × 20%)	312
Impaired debt relief (£1,760 × 20%)	352
	22,348

> *Tutorial note*
>
> *VAT can be recovered on entertaining overseas customers but not UK customers.*
>
> *VAT cannot be recovered on cars unless they are used 100% for business.*

(W3) Purchases and other inputs

	£
Purchases	113,670
Purchase returns	(5,249)
Car	14,000
Entertaining overseas customers	1,560
	123,981

45 DENZIL DYER

(a) Identification of the type of supply

- Output VAT is only due in respect of standard rated supplies. Incorrectly classifying a supply as zero rated would not remove Denzil's liability to pay the output VAT which is calculated on the actual price charged. This would then be an additional cost to the business.

- The type of supply, whether standard rated or zero rated, has no effect on the recovery of input VAT for Denzil.

(b) VAT implications of discounts

- Where a discount of 5% is given for an order of more than £500 then output VAT is simply calculated on the revised, discounted, selling price.

- As regards the 2.5% discount offered for prompt payment, output VAT is calculated on the amount that the customer actually pays.

- For prompt payment discounts the supplier will not know, when the invoice is raised, whether the customer will qualify for the discount by paying within the required timescale.

The supplier must therefore charge VAT on the invoice on the full price and either issue a credit note if the discount is taken or adjust their records to account for output tax on the amount received when the invoice is paid.

(c) **Conditions for the recovery of input VAT**

- The supply must be made to Denzil since he is the taxable person making the claim.

- The supply must be supported by evidence, normally in the form of a VAT invoice. Denzil will therefore not be able to recover any input VAT in respect of the purchases of office supplies for cash, where there is no invoice.

- Denzil must use the goods or services supplied for business purposes, although an apportionment can be made where supplies are acquired partly for business purposes and partly for private purposes.

(d) **Circumstances for issuing VAT invoices**

- Denzil must issue a VAT invoice when he makes a standard rated supply to one of his VAT registered customers.

- A VAT invoice is not required if the supply is zero rated or the supply is to a non-VAT registered customer (e.g. a member of the public) then an invoice need not be issued unless the customer requests.

- A simplified invoice can be issued if the supply is less than £250.

- A VAT invoice should be issued within 30 days of the date that the supply of services is treated as being made.

46 VARDY PLC

(a) **Default surcharge**

- Vardy plc has already defaulted twice during the current default surcharge period, so a further default will result in a surcharge of 10% of the amount of VAT outstanding.

- In addition, the default surcharge period will be extended to the 12-month anniversary of the VAT quarter to which the default relates.

- In order to revert to a clean default surcharge record, Vardy plc will need to submit four consecutive VAT returns on time and also pay the related VAT liabilities on time.

(b) **Errors on a VAT return and default interest**

- Vardy plc will be permitted to disclose the underpayment of VAT of £8,200 by entering this amount on its next VAT return as the net error is less than the limit of £10,000.

- Default interest is not charged where voluntary disclosure can be made by entering the underpayment on the next VAT return.

(c) **VAT penalties**

- Vardy plc has been careless in its incorrect treatment of the supply of services received, so the maximum amount of penalty will therefore be 30% of the VAT underpaid (£8,200 × 30% = £2,460).

- However, this penalty could be reduced to £0 as a result of the company's unprompted disclosure to HM Revenue and Customs.

TASK 1.3

47   NON-CURRENT ASSETS 1

Narrative	Dr	Cr
Disposals	**12,000**	
Vehicles at cost		**12,000**
Vehicles accumulated depreciation	**9,119**	
Disposals		**9,119**
Vehicles at cost	**15,250**	
Motor vehicle expenses	**210**	
Disposals		**3,800**
Sundry payables		**11,660**
Totals	**36,579**	**36,579**

48   NON-CURRENT ASSETS 2

(a)   Year ended 31/12/X1 £20,000 × 10% = £2,000

Year ended 31/12/X2 (£20,000 – £2,000) × 10% = £1,800

Year ended 31/12/X3 (£20,000 – £2,000 – £1,800) × 10% = £1,620

Total accumulated depreciation (£2,000 + £1,800 + £1,620) = £5,420

(b)

Narrative	Dr	Cr
Disposals account	20,000	
Machinery cost account		20,000
Machinery accumulated depreciation account	5,420	
Disposals account		5,420
Bank	10,000	
VAT Control (20/120 × £10,000)		1,667
Disposals account (100/120 × £10,000)		8,333
Totals	35,420	35,420

Disposals

Machinery at cost	20,000	Machinery accumulated depreciation	5,420
		Bank	8,333
		Loss on disposal	6,247
	20,000		20,000

The profit or loss on disposal can also be calculated by comparing the sales proceeds to the carrying amount. The sales proceeds are £8,333 compared to a carrying amount of £14,580.

Therefore, a loss of £6,247 has been made.

49   YEAR-END 1

(a)

	£	*Debit*	*Credit*
Accruals	4,820		4,820
Prepayments	2,945	2,945	
Motor expenses	572	572	
Administration expenses	481	481	
Light and heat	1,073	1,073	
Revenue	48,729		48,729
Purchases	26,209	26,209	
SLCA	5,407	5,407	
PLCA	3,090		3,090
Rent	45	45	
Purchase returns	306		306
Discounts allowed	567	567	
Capital	10,000		10,000
Loan	15,000		15,000
Interest paid	750	750	
Drawings	4,770	4,770	
Motor vehicles – cost	19,000	19,000	
Motor vehicle – acc. depreciation	2,043		2,043
VAT control	2,995		2,995
Wages	20,000	20,000	
Suspense account		**5,164**	
Totals		86,983	86,983

(b)

		Dr £	Cr £
(i)	Suspense	5,000	
	Capital		5,000
(ii)	Suspense	385	
	Sales ledger control account		385
(iii)	VAT	193	
	Suspense		193
(iv)	Rent	4,500	
	Suspense		4,500
	Rent	4,500	
	Suspense		4,500
(v)	Electricity	1,356	
	Suspense		1,356

50   ETB 1

Extended trial balance

Ledger account	Ledger balances		Adjustments	
	Dr £	Cr £	Dr £	Cr £
Accruals		1,330		300
Advertising	1,800			
Bank	7,912			
Capital		50,000		
Closing inventory			11,890	11,890
Depreciation charge				
Drawings	14,700			
Fixtures and fittings – accumulated depreciation		945		
Fixtures and fittings – cost	6,099			
Irrecoverable debts	345			
Allowance for doubtful debt adjustment				295
Electricity	1,587		300	
Loan	10,000			
Opening inventory	5,215			
Prepayment			12,500	
Allowance for doubtful debts		485	295	
Purchases	78,921			
Purchase returns				2,000
PLCA		14,000	2,400	
Rent	25,000			12,500
Revenue		145,825		
SLCA	9,500			
VAT control account		11,453		400
Wages	62,959			
	224,038	224,038	27,385	27,385

Key answer tips

(a)   SLCA 9,500 × 2% = 190. Allowance currently 485, therefore debit with £295 to make it equal £190

(c)   The prepayment for the year end is 10/12 × 15,000 = 12,500. For November and December X5 = 2/12 × 15,000 = 2,500. Total rental charge for the year = (10/12 × 12,000) + 2,500 = £12,500

(e)   Accrual for November and December. 2/3 × 450 = £300

51 ETB 2

Extended trial balance

Ledger account	Ledger balances		Adjustments		Statement of profit or loss		Statement of financial position	
	Dr £	Cr £	Dr £	Cr £	Dr £	Cr £	Dr £	Cr £
Accruals		2,300		425				2,725
Advertising	1,800				1,800			
Bank	7,912		1,175				9,087	
Capital		40,000						40,000
Closing inventory			6,590	6,590		6,590	6,590	
Depreciation charge			821		821			
Drawings	14,700						14,700	
Fixtures and fittings – accumulated depreciation		945		821				1,766
Fixtures and fittings – cost	6,099						6,099	
Interest	345				345			
Light and heat	1,587		706		2,293			
Loan		10,000						10,000
Opening inventory	5,215				5,215			
Prepayments	485		927	281			1,131	
Purchases	75,921				75,921			
PLCA		14,000						14,000
Rent and rates	38,000			927	37,073			
Revenue		145,825				145,825		
SLCA	9,500			1,175			8,325	
VAT control account		11,453						11,453
Wages	62,959				62,959			
Loss						34,012	34,012	
	224,523	224,523	10,219	10,219	186,427	186,427	79,944	79,944

52   INCOMPLETE 1

(a)   £55,200

(b)   **Receivables (Sales ledger) control account**

Balance b/d	4,120	Bank	53,610
Credit sales	55,200	Balance c/d	5,710
	59,320		59,320

(c)   £254,400

(d)   **Bank account**

Balance b/d	5,630	Payroll expenses	48,000
SLCA	53,610	Administration expenses	6,400
Cash sales	254,400	Vehicle running costs	192,000
		Drawings	41,800
		Sales tax	17,300
		Balance c/d	8,140
	313,640		313,640

53   INCOMPLETE 2

£4,000

54   INCOMPLETE 3

(a)   £1,280,000 × 75/100 = £960,000

(b)   £960,000 − (£970,200 − £98,006) = £87,806

55 SOLE TRADER 1

Vincent Trading			
Statement of financial position as at 30 June 20X8			
	£	£	£
Non-current assets	**Cost**	**Depreciation**	**Carrying amount**
Equipment	17,500	4,500	13,000
Current assets			
Inventory		7,850	
Trade receivables (£7,800 – £840)		6,960	
Prepayments		3,200	
		18,010	
Current liabilities			
Payables (£6,800 + £1,450)	8,250		
VAT	2,950		
Accruals	750		
Bank	1,250		
		13,200	
Net current assets			4,810
Net assets			17,810
Financed by:			
Opening capital			17,000
Add: Net profit			8,810
Less: Drawings			8,000
Closing capital			17,810

56 SOLE TRADER 2

Beale – Statement of financial position as at 30 June 20X6			
	£	£	£
Non-current assets	Cost	Depreciation	Carrying amount
Motor vehicles	45,000	20,000	25,000
Current assets			
Inventory		17,500	
Trade receivables (£68,550 – £1,450)		67,100	
Cash		500	
		85,100	
Current liabilities			
Bank	2,250		
Trade payables	23,750		
Accruals	3,150		
VAT	3,500		
		32,650	
Net current assets			52,450
Net assets			77,450
Financed by:			
Opening capital			85,000
Less: Net loss			4,350
Less: Drawings			3,200
Closing capital			77,450

57 PARTNER 1

Partnership appropriation account for the year ended 30 June 20X9

	£
Profit for the year	220,000
Salaries:	
Gertrude	−18,000
Eddie	0
Polonius	−36,000
Interest on capital:	
Gertrude	−2,000
Eddie	−2,000
Polonius	−2,000
Sales commission:	
Gertrude	−8,250
Eddie	−6,800
Polonius	−4,715
Profit available for distribution	140,235
Profit share:	
Gertrude(40% × £140,235)	56,094
Ed (40% × £140,235)	56,094
Polonius (20% × £140,235)	28,047
Total residual profit distributed	140,235

58 PARTNER 2

(a)

Account name	Dr	Cr
Goodwill	£105,000	
Capital account – Cordelia		£36,750
Capital account – Goneril		£68,250

(b) £31,750

New goodwill value = £105,000 + £22,000

= £127,000

× 25% = £31,750

59   PARTNER 3

Capital account – Will

Bank	31,000	Balance b/d	9,000
		Goodwill	15,000
		Current account	7,000
	31,000		31,000

60   COSTING 1

(a)   **£10,800**

Using FIFO, inventory is issued at the earliest price.

The issue on the 19 January would be made up of 500 costing		1,250
	1,000 costing	2,750
	600 × 2.80	1,680
The issue on the 31 January would be made up of 1,000 × 2.80		2,800
	800 × 2.90	2,320

Total issue value   **£10,800**

(b)   **£5,120**

Using LIFO, the 1,900 units of closing inventory is valued as the opening inventory of 500 units (£1,250) plus the 1,000 units received on 4 January (£2,750) plus 400 of the units received on 11 January, which have a value of £4,480 × 400/1,600 = £1,120.

	£
400 units of opening inventory	1,250
1,000 units received on 4 January	2,750
400 units received on 11 January	1,120
Total value of closing inventory	**5,120**

(c)   £2.83

With cumulative weighted average cost method, a new average cost only needs to be calculated before there is an issue from stores.

	Units	Total cost £	Average cost £
Opening inventory	500	1,250	
Receipts on 4 January	1,000	2,750	
Receipts on 11 January	1,600	4,480	
Receipts on 18 January	1,200	3,480	
	4,300	11,960	£2.78
B/f	4,300	11,960	£2.78
Issues on 19 January	(2,100)	(5,838)	£2.78
	2,200	6,122	
Receipts on 25 January	1,500	4,350	
	3,700	10,472	**£2.83**
Issues on 31 January	(1,800)	(5,094)	**£2.83**
	1,900	5,378	

61   COSTING 2

Characteristic	FIFO	LIFO	AVCO
Potentially out of date valuation on issues.	✓		
The valuation of inventory rarely reflects the actual purchase price of the material.			✓
Potentially out of date closing inventory valuation.		✓	
This inventory valuation method is particularly suited to inventory that consist of liquid materials e.g. oil.			✓
This inventory valuation method is particularly suited to inventory that has a short shelf life e.g. dairy products.	✓		
This inventory valuation method is suited to a wheat farmer who has large silos of grain. Grain is added to and taken from the top of these silos.		✓	
In times of rising prices this method will give higher profits.	✓		
In times of rising prices this method will give lower profits.		✓	
In times of rising prices this method gives a middle level of profits compared to the other two.			✓
Issues are valued at the most recent purchase cost.		✓	
Inventory is valued at the average of the cost of purchases.			✓
Inventory is valued at the most recent purchase cost.	✓		

62 COSTING 3

Cost	Direct	Indirect
Basic pay for production workers	✓	
Supervisors wages		✓
Bonus for salesman		✓
Production workers overtime premium due to general pressures		✓
Holiday pay for production workers		✓
Sick pay for supervisors		✓
Time spent by production workers cleaning the machinery		✓

63 COSTING 4

(a)

	Units
Actual production	5,400,000
Standard production (5,000 hours at 800 units)	(4,000,000)
Excess production	1,400,000
Bonus %	$\dfrac{25\% \times 1,400,000}{4,000.000} = 8.75\%$
Group bonus rate per hour	0.0875 × £10 = £0.875
Total group bonus	5,000 hours at £0.875 = £4,375

(b) Basic pay 44 hours at £9.60 =   £422.40

Bonus pay 44 hours at £0.875 =   £38.50

Total pay   **£460.90**

64 COSTING 5

Description	Units	Unit cost £	Total cost £	Description	Units	Unit cost £	Total cost £
Input – Statues	300	11.25	3,375	Normal loss	30	5.00	150
Materials – Glaze			500	Output	290	49.35	14,312
Labour			5,760				
Overheads			3,840				
Abnormal gain	20	49.35	987				
	320		14,462		320		14,462

65 COSTING 6

Note: Using AVCO so the EU calculation will include all costs (including those b/f in OWIP) and all output, not just the work done this period.

Equivalent units		Material	Conversion
	Completed output	3,200	3,200
	Total EU	3,200	3,200
Costs	OWIP	53,800	42,000
	Period	135,000	98,800
	Total cost	188,800	140,800
Cost per EU		59	44

66 OVERHEADS 1

	Basis of apportionment	Scheduled routes	Charter services	Maintenance and repairs	Fuel/ parts	General Admin	Totals
		£000	£000	£000	£000	£000	£000
Depreciation of vehicles	NBV of vehicles	21,840	14,560	–	–	–	36,400
Fuel and other variables	Planned mileage	23,210	18,990	–	–	–	42,200
Driver salaries	Allocated	5,250	4,709	–	–	–	9,959
Rent and rates and other premises costs	Floor space	–	–	6,300	3,780	2,520	12,600
Indirect labour	Allocated	–	–	9,600	3,200	7,800	20,600
Totals		**50,300**	**38,259**	**15,900**	**6,980**	**10,320**	**121,759**
Reapportion Maintenance and repairs		9,540	6,360	(15,900)			
Reapportion fuel and parts store		3,839	3,141		(6,980)		
Reapportion General Admin		5,160	5,160			(10,320)	
Total to profit centres		68,839	52,920				121,759

67 OVERHEADS 2

(a) £35.00

$$\text{Overhead absorption rate} = \frac{\text{Total overhead cost}}{\text{Total number of direct labour hours}}$$

Total overhead cost = 90,000 + 150,000 + 180,000 = £420,000

Total direct labour hours = (5 × 1,200) + (5 × 10,800) = 60,000 direct labour hours

Overhead absorption rate = £420,000 ÷ 60,000 direct labour hours

Overhead absorption rate = £7.00 per labour hour

Alpha uses 5 direct labour hours per unit so will have an overhead cost per unit of 5 hours × £7.00 per hour = £35.00.

(b) £35.00

The overhead cost per unit for each unit of product Beta will be the same as product Alpha, as both products use the same number of labour hours (5 hours).

(c) £125.83

	Labour related	*Purchasing related*	*Set-up related*
Costs	£90,000	£150,000	£180,000
Consumption of activities (cost drivers)	60,000 labour hours	150 purchase orders	100 set-ups
Cost per unit of cost driver	£1.50 per labour hour	£1,000 per purchase order	£1,800 per set-up
Costs per product			
Product Alpha:	£1.50 × 6,000 labour hours = £ 9,000	£1,000 × 70 purchase orders = £ 70,000	£1,800 × 40 set-ups = £72,000
Product Beta:	£1.50 × 54,000 labour hours = £ 81,000	£1,000 × 80 purchase orders = £80,000	£1,800 × 60 set-ups = £108,000

Total overhead cost for Alpha = £9,000 + £70,000 + £72,000 = £151,000. Spread over 1,200 units, this represents a cost per unit of £125.83.

(d) £24.91

Total overhead cost for Beta = £81,000 + £80,000 + £108,000 = £269,000. Spread over 10,800 units, this represents a cost per unit of £24.91.

68 OVERHEADS 3

Marginal costing

	£000	£000
Sales		50,000
Opening inventory	0	
Production costs (7,560 + 17,640)	25,200	
Closing inventory (25,200/1,800 × 800)	−11,200	
Cost of sales		−14,000
Contribution		36,000
Fixed costs (3,600 + 2,010)		−5,610
Profit for the period		30,390

Absorption costing

	£000	£000
Sales		50,000
Opening inventory	0	
Production costs (7,560 + 17,640 + 3,600)	28,800	
Closing inventory (28,800/1,800 × 800)	−12,800	
Cost of sales		−16,000
Gross Profit		34,000
Non-production cost		−2,010
Profit for the period		31,990

69 DECISIONS 1

	Notes	£
Bricks 400,000 @ $120 per thousand	1	48,000
Other material	2	5,000
Skilled labour 2,400 × $12	3	38,400
Unskilled labour	4	–
Scaffolding hire	5	3,500
Depreciation	6	–
Rental cost of yard	7	10,000
Plans	8	–
Profit	9	–
		107,300

Notes:

(1)   Bricks are in regular use and will have to be replaced therefore the relevant cost is the replacement cost.

(2)   Other materials are bought in for the job and are an incremental cost.

(3)   Skilled labour is hired in and is therefore an incremental cost.

(4)   Unskilled labour is currently idle and would be paid anyway.

(5)   Scaffolding hire is an incremental cost.

(6)   Depreciation is a notional cost and therefore not relevant.

(7)   The lost revenue of using the yard is an incremental cost of £500 × 20.

(8)   Sunk cost so not relevant.

(9)   The lowest price is required so this would be at the breakeven level.

70   DECISIONS 2

(a)   **CVP analysis**

			Present	*Proposed*
(i)	Breakeven point			
	Units: $\dfrac{\text{Fixed costs}}{\text{Contribution p.u.}}$		$\dfrac{96{,}000}{(1.70-1.40)}$	$\dfrac{130{,}000}{(1.60-1.35)}$
			= 320,000 units	= 520,000 units
	Revenue: × 1.70/1.60		£544,000	£832,000
(ii)	Annual profit			
	Sales units		500,000	750,000
	Contribution per unit		£0.30	£0.25
			£	£
	Total contribution		150,000	187,500
	Fixed costs		96,000	130,000
	Profit		54,000	57,500
(iii)	Margin of safety ratio			
	$\dfrac{\text{Budgeted units}-\text{breakeven}}{\text{Budgeted units}}$		$\dfrac{500-320}{500}$	$\dfrac{750-520}{750}$
			= 0.36 (36%)	= 0.307 (30.7%)

(b)   **Advice to Dilemma**

Looking at the figures alone, the advice to Dilemma would be to proceed with the proposed expansion, as it is projected to increase annual profits by £3,500, i.e. 6.5%.

However, it should be noted that the margin of safety ratio (the relative amount by which sales can fall below budget before making a loss) will fall from 36% to 30.7%.

This means that the business is more vulnerable to downturns in the market.

71 DECISIONS 3

(a)

		Product			
	A	B	C	D	Total
Selling price	100	110	120	120	
Variable cost per unit	54	55	59	66	
Contribution/unit	£46.00	£55.00	£61.00	£54.00	
Hours/unit $\left(\dfrac{\text{Direct labour cost}}{£6/\text{hour}}\right)$	3.00	2.50	4.00	4.50	
Contribution/hour	£15.33	£22.00	£15.25	£12.00	
Ranking	2nd	1st	3rd	4th	

	A	B	C	D	Total
We *must* produce 20 litres of each which uses (hours)	60	50	80	90	280

The balance of hours are allocated according to rankings, subject to maximum demand levels

Product B first

(150 – 20) = 130 litres		325 hours			325
					605

Then Product A

(200 – 20) = 180 litres	540 hours				540
					1,145

Then Product C

(100 – 20) = 80 litres, but we only have time for 200/4 = 50 litres			200 hours		200
					1,345

The production plan is thus:

A	200 litres
B	150 litres
C	70 litres
D	20 litres

The contribution is:

		£
A	200 litres × £46	9,200
B	150 litres × £55	8,250
C	70 litres × £61	4,270
D	20 litres × £54	1,080
		22,800
Less:	Fixed overhead (1,600 hours × £8)	12,800
	Profit	10,000

Note: The hourly rate for fixed overhead is calculated from product costs (e.g. for A: $\dfrac{£24}{3\,hours}$ = £8 per hour).

72 DECISIONS 4

	Year 0 £000	Year 1 £000	Year 2 £000	Year 3 £000
Capital expenditure	−500			
Sales income		280	330	370
Operating costs		−100	−120	−140
Net cash flows	−500	180	210	230
PV factors	1.0000	0.909	0.826	0.751
Discounted cash flows	−500	164	173	173
Net present value	10			

(a) The net present value is **positive** £10,000.

(b) **D** – given the NPV is positive, the IRR must be greater than the cost of capital used of 10%.

(c)

Year	Cash flow £000	Cumulative cash flow £000
0	(500)	(500)
1	180	(320)
2	210	(110)
3	230	120

The payback period is **2** years and **6** months.

Months = 110/230 × 12 = 5.7 months.

TASK 1.4

73   AVOIDANCE

Both tax evasion and tax avoidance are illegal, but tax evasion involves providing HM Revenue and Customs with deliberately false information	
Tax evasion is illegal, whereas tax avoidance involves the minimisation of tax liabilities by the use of any lawful means	✓
Both tax evasion and tax avoidance are illegal, but tax avoidance involves providing HM Revenue and Customs with deliberately false information	
Tax avoidance is illegal, whereas tax evasion involves the minimisation of tax liabilities by the use of any lawful means	

Tutorial note

The term tax evasion summarises any action taken to avoid or reduce tax by illegal means, for example providing HM Revenue and Customs with deliberately false information.

74   DUMPING

Members have a duty of confidentiality.

However, there are occasions where the accountant has a professional or legal duty to disclose the information and therefore the breach of confidentiality is permissible.

Environmental damage is one such instance.

75   INTEGRITY

Appropriate responses include the following:

Internal action

- Discuss the matter with the Finance Director to see if there is a valid case for posting this journal. From the information given, this seems unlikely.

External action

If the FD refuses to change the request and Frankie still feels uncomfortable, then he could:

- Go to the company's auditors to discuss the matter

- Seek guidance from the AAT .

Ultimately if the situation is not resolved, then he should consider resigning.

Note: The wrong answer here is to suggest that he should post the journal without question as the Finance director is his senior. This is NOT an appropriate action.

76 BENEFITS

(a) The ethical principles potentially affected are as follows:

Integrity – How will Jacqui manage her personal interest with the need to be true and fair?

Objectivity – How will Jacqui manage her personal interest in the benefits package with the need to remain unbiased and consider only the relevant facts?

Professional Competence and Due Care – Does Jacqui have all the necessary skills to draw up such a package?

Professional Behaviour – How should Jacqui proceed so as not to bring discredit herself and the accountancy profession?

It would be very easy for Jacqui's recommendations to appear biased, even if she has acted ethically.

(b) Jacqui should start by considering the following issues:

Identify relevant facts:

She should consider the organisation's policies, procedures and guidelines, accounting standards, best practices, code of ethics, applicable laws and regulations.

Is the information used for assessing the potential new benefits package independent? Who else has been involved in the proposal for the new benefits package?

Identify affected parties:

Key affected parties are Jacqui and the rest of the SMT. Other possible affected parties are employees, human resources, shareholders and financial backers.

Identify who should be involved in the resolution:

Jacqui should consider not just who should be involved, but also for what reason and timing of their involvement.

She could think about contacting the AAT for advice and guidance, or discuss the matter with trusted colleagues or someone from human resources.

(c) **Possible courses of action**

Before explaining her findings to the SMT, it may be advisable for Jacqui to tell the SMT how she approached the project and who else was involved, for example, human resources.

She should declare her conflict of interest and not vote on the proposal for the new benefits package.

It may be advisable to involve human resources or another independent party to present the findings to the SMT. During the presentation, she should demonstrate how her findings were arrived at and who else was involved in the project.

77 SUSHIL

(a) This situation presents an intimidation threat.

(b) The best course of action would be to speak to his employer and explain that it is illegal to falsify the accounts.

78 TRUE

(a) No, Naills as an AAT member has a duty to produce a true and fair view of the accounts.

(b) The definition of false accounting is concealing or falsifying accounting records with a view to personal gain or providing false information that is misleading or deceptive.

79 MEERA

Matter 1

(a) Fees

While some discounting of fees is seen as commercially acceptable way to win business, heavily discounted fees are perceived as a 'self-interest' threat to professional behaviour. This does not mean that they should be avoided at all costs but guidelines need to be followed.

Fees should reflect the value of the professional services performed for the client and there is a risk with low fees of a perception that the quality of work could be impaired.

Tax bill

Meera should consider the fundamental principle of Integrity.

It would be dishonest to promise to reduce a tax bill simply to gain a client when she believes the bill to be reasonable.

Matter 2

(b) Meera should continue to advise Greg to contact the HMRC but it would be a breach of confidentiality for her to do so without his express permission, which seems unlikely in this case.

(c) If Greg, after having had a reasonable time to reflect, does not correct the error, Meera should do the following:

- Inform Greg that she/her firm can no longer act for him because funds dishonestly retained after discovery of a tax error become criminal property so their retention amounts to money laundering by Greg.

- Make an internal report on the matter to her firm's MLRO.

80 RS

(a) The fundamental principles of integrity and objectivity are being threated here. Changing the management information would breach both of these principles.

(b) The offers of incentives make this a self-interest threat as RS stands to benefit if he/she changes the figures.

81 DISMISS

The Public Interest Disclosure Act 1998 (PIDA) protects individuals from dismissal who disclose confidential information, whether internally or to a prescribed regulator when given in good faith.

Sarah is thus protected under the PIDA.

82 SUSTENANCE

(a) The role of accountants

The roles of professional accountants in contributing to sustainability include the following:

- Challenging conventional assumptions of doing business.
- Redefining success.
- Establishing appropriate performance targets.
- Encouraging and rewarding the right behaviours.
- Ensuring that information flows that support decisions, and which monitor and report performance, go beyond the traditional ways of thinking about economic success.

Being sustainable requires the organisation to take full account of its impact on the planet and its people.

(b) Impact on profit

An increased emphasis on sustainability can result in improved profits for the following reasons:

- Potential cost savings – e.g. due to lower energy usage.
- Short term gain in sales – e.g. if customers are influenced by sustainability-related labels on products.
- Long term gain in sales – e.g. due to enhanced PR and reputation.
- Better risk management – e.g. pre-empting changes in regulations may save compliance costs.

83 TIO RINO

Mining companies can try to be sustainable by adopting the following:

Social issues ('people')

- Provide a safe and healthy workplace for employees where their rights and dignity are respected.
- Build enduring relationships with local communities and neighbours that demonstrate mutual respect, active partnership, and long-term commitment.
- Improve safety record re accident, fatalities.
- Develop health programmes for local communities – e.g. in respect of AIDS/HIV in some African countries.
- Ensure that if communities need to be moved or relocated, that resettlement and compensation are generous and cultural heritage is not compromised.
- Invest in people over the long term by fostering diversity, providing challenging and exciting work and development opportunities, and rewarding for performance.
- Ensure post-mining land use is discussed with local communities and is consistent with their aims and needs.

Environmental issues ('planet')

- Wherever possible prevent – or otherwise minimise, mitigate and remediate – harmful effects of activities on the environment.

- Avoid developing sites where the risk to biodiversity is particularly high.

- Develop new ways to reduce emissions of dangerous gases such as SO_2 and NO_2.

- Plant new trees elsewhere to replace ones felled for mining to ensure biodiversity.

- Landscape and replant sites after mining has finished. Pay for species to be repopulated.

- Use offsetting schemes to compensate for emission of greenhouse gases (e.g. schemes to plant additional trees somewhere else).

- Develop ways to process waste to avoid polluting the surrounding water system.

- Reducing energy usage by more efficient processes.

- Recycle as much waste products as possible.

Economic issues ('Profit')

- Pay taxes without finding loopholes to avoid them.

- Ensure local communities benefit in terms of employments and a share of overall profits.

- Reinvest in local communities and projects rather than taking all profits back to the mining company's home country.

84 HOGGS FURNITURE

(a) Sustainable development is defined as 'development that meets the needs of the present without compromising the ability of future generations to meet their own needs' *(The UN's Bruntland Report).*

Sustainability is thus more than just looking at environmental concerns. It relates to the continuity of **economic**, **social** and **environmental** aspects of human society.

Another way of looking at this is that sustainable businesses offer products and services that fulfil society's needs while placing an equal emphasis on people, planet and profits.

(b) Areas that Jacob should appraise in order to answer the client's concerns include the following:

- Whether non-renewable hard woods are used in manufacture.

    The client would want reassurance that all materials are form renewable sources.

- The energy efficiency and level of emission of greenhouse gases due to the operation of the factory.

    While these cannot be eliminated altogether, the client would want to see evidence that Hoggs has taken steps to improve energy efficiency (e.g. thermal insulation, double glazing, installation of solar panels, etc) or uses carbon offset schemes.

- Treatment of staff

  Sustainability is not just about environmental issues but also incorporates social (people) aspects. The client may want to know what Hoggs' record is concerning accidents, staff development, diversity, etc.

- Tax

  Economic sustainability includes factors such as whether the company is paying tax and so contributing to the local/national community.

(c) Other ways Jacob can contribute to sustainability through his role as an accountant includes the following:

- Helping create an ethics-based culture in Hoggs.

- By championing and promoting sustainability.

- By highlighting the risks of not acting sustainably and draw attention to reputational and other ethical risks.

- By incorporating targets and performance measures consistent with a Triple Bottom Line (TBL) approach.

85 MLC

MLC have clearly positioned themselves as an ethical company and will therefore attract shareholders who are looking for ethical investments and customers looking for ethically produced goods.

If they continue trading with this supplier then their reputation will suffer if the news gets out.

By taking strong decisive action and controlling the news story they have demonstrated that they follow their stated ethical principles.

The best response would thus be to "Cancel all contracts with the supplier and release a press statement stating how the company will always act quickly and decisively if unethical practices are suspected."

86   STEPHANIE

Integrity

Integrity implies that a person should be straightforward and honest in all business relationships. The management accountant is not being honest because he is helping to produce budgets he knows to be inaccurate.

Objectivity

By taking the football tickets in exchange for altering figures the management accountant is allowing bias to override business judgements.

Professional competence and due care

The management accountant's skills are not under question and so this principle does not appear to have been breached.

Confidentiality

The management accountant does not appear to have breached confidentiality. The conversations Stephanie overheard involved Alpha staff and so no information has been leaked.

Professional behaviour

The management accountant has not behaved professionally and in line with AAT expectations. In addition to using incorrect figures in the budgets he has tried to influence Stephanie to do the same.

87   STEVEN

In respect of a genuine oversight, be it yours or a colleague's, AAT's code of ethics recognises that this can happen as long as the issue is promptly addressed and safeguards put in place.

It is possible to add an addendum about the incorrect note and this is the most expedient action.

However, it would be advisable first to consult with N&Q's auditors for their guidance on how best to proceed.

If the accounts do not "represent the facts accurately and completely in all material respects" you should not sign them, nor should the MD.

Section 4

ANSWERS TO EXAM – PART II PRACTICE TASKS

The answers to the tasks in these scenarios can be found as spreadsheet files on your MyKaplan account (together with the text and word files required).

Please go to www.mykaplan.co.uk and login using your username and password.

Section 5

MOCK ASSESSMENT – QUESTIONS

PART 1

TASK 1.1   (15 marks)

This task is based on a workplace scenario separate to the rest of the assessment.

An accountant, Siobahn, has recently started work at Plug Ltd, a large organisation with many employees. She mainly works in the accounts department and is currently responsible for performing bank reconciliations and control account reconciliations. She is trying to apply the ethical code's conceptual framework to some ethical problems she is facing at work and is currently evaluating threats to her fundamental principles.

(a)   Are these statements true or false?   **(2 marks)**

Statement	True	False
The AAT code of ethics gives detailed rules that cover a wide range of possible scenarios.		
Some of the ethical principles can be overlooked if it is in the public interest to do so.		

(b)   For each of the following scenarios identify the nature of the ethical threat.   **(2 marks)**

Scenario	Threat
Siobahn is seconded to internal audit and asked to verify that control procedures have been followed correctly, including bank reconciliations.	
Siobahn's brother is one of Plug Ltd's suppliers.	

∇ Drop down list for task 1.1 (b)

Self-interest threat
Self-review threat
Advocacy threat
Familiarity threat
Intimidation threat

An ex-boyfriend of Siobahn is demanding that she reveal confidential information about Plug Ltd's manufacturing processes or he will publish compromising photographs of her online.

(c) **Identify whether the following statements are true or false.** **(3 marks)**

Statement	True	False
Siobahn may never disclose confidential information to any third party.		
The threat that Siobahn is facing to her compliance with the fundamental principles is a self-interest threat.		
Siobahn must resign immediately from Plug Ltd as her integrity has been compromised by her past relationships.		

Terry is also an accountant as Plug Ltd and often helps the sales department when pitching for new contracts. Whilst pitching for a contract in the local area, Plug Ltd was competing against the main rival local firm. The competitor firm is in serious financial difficulties and approached Terry to offer him an all-expenses paid holiday in return for offering a more expensive price to the potential client. It turns out that the competitor would have gone into administration without this contract win. James has been unsure as to whether he should accept the offer.

(d) **Complete the following statement.** **(2 marks)**

Being offered gifts by the rival firm is [▽] to Terry's fundamental

principle of [▽]

▽ Drop down list for task 1.1 (d)

a self-interest threat
a familiarity threat
objectivity
professional competence

Terry has decided not to accept the holiday and inflate his recommended price, despite his belief that Plug Ltd was unlikely to win the tender anyway.

(e) **Identify whether the following statements are true or false.** **(3 marks)**

Statement	True	False
Had he accepted the holiday, Terry would have been guilty of the offence of 'active' bribery under the UK Bribery Act (2010).		
The UK Bribery Act (2010) only applies to UK citizens, residents and companies established under UK law.		
Not all gifts or hospitality would be considered to be bribes.		

Recently Bath plc, a customer of Plug Ltd, sent in a cheque for £80,000 in payment of an invoice for £8,000. When Terry queried this, the client said it was a mistake and asked for a cheque for the difference of £72,000 to be written to Faucet plc, a sister company of Bath plc.

(f)   Identify whether the following statements are true or false.   **(3 marks)**

Statement	True	False
Terry should report the matter to the firm's MRLO.		
Plug Ltd should scrutinise the request carefully before agreeing to any payment.		
Unless investigations satisfy any concerns raised, then the MRLO should fill in a Suspicious Activity Report (SAR) to be sent to the NCA.		

TASK 1.2   **(16 marks)**

This task is based on the workplace scenario of Ovey and Sach.

You are Tina Jeffrey, a part-qualified Accounting Technician. You work for Ovey and Sach, a business which makes and sells designer gifts. Ovey and Sach is a partnership owned by Mike Ovey and Andrew Sach.

You cover all aspects of bookkeeping and accounting for the business. Other accountants working at Ovey and Sach are Graham Hyde, another part-qualified technician and Susan Wright, the chief accountant.

Ovey and Sach makes standard-rated and zero-rated supplies but is not yet registered for VAT.

The date is 1 March 20X6. Sales details are as follows:

	Monthly turnover	
	Standard-rated	Zero-rated
	£	£
Year ended 31 December 20X5 (Actual)	2,000	4,000
January 20X6 (Actual)	2,500	3,100
February 20X6 (Actual)	6,500	4,600
March 20X6 (Forecast)	7,900	5,200
April 20X6 and thereafter (Forecast)	8,700	5,900

(a)   At the end of which month does Ovey and Sach exceed the registration threshold?
                                                                    (2 marks)

February 20X6	
March 20X6	
April 20X6	
December 20X6	

Mike Ovey is considering registering the business for VAT voluntarily rather than waiting until the taxable turnover is over the registration threshold. Andrew Sach is less convinced and wants your views on the subject.

(b) **Identify which of the following reasons might explain why a business would NOT voluntarily register for VAT?** **(4 marks)**

Statement	True	False
It makes their goods more expensive for other VAT-registered businesses.		
It makes their goods more expensive for businesses that are not VAT-registered.		
It helps to avoid penalties for late registration.		
It increases the business burden of administration.		

Today's date is now 30 June 20X6 and Ovey and Sach is now a VAT-registered business.

On 4 May Ovey and Sach receives an order for goods from a customer. On 15 May the goods are delivered and on 20 May you issue a tax invoice. The customer pays on 28 June.

(c) **What is the tax point date?** **(2 marks)**

4 May 20X6	
15 May 20X6	
20 May 20X6	
28 June 20X6	

Ovey and Sach's VAT account at 30 September, the end of its last VAT period, is as follows:

		£			£
			30/06	Balance b/d	4,561.02
30/09	Purchases day book	4,532.25	30/09	Sales day book	5,587.32
30/09	Sales returns day book	785.69	30/09	Purchases returns day book	403.68
30/09	Balance c/d	5,234.08			
		10,552.02			10,552.02

(d) **What figure will be inserted in Box 1 of the VAT return for the VAT period ended 30 September 20X6?** **(1 mark)**

£ [ ]

On reviewing Ovey and Sach's day books, you have found two errors:

- Input VAT of £56.50 on a purchases invoice was wrongly recorded as purchases on 29 July.

- A sales invoice for a zero rated supply of £500 (net) had been entered twice in the sales day book.

You prepare journals to correct these errors.

(e) **Once the journals have been processed, what will be the revised balance carried down on the VAT account?** **(2 marks)**

£ [   ]

It is now 14 October. You have just received an invoice from Briggs Ltd where the VAT has been incorrectly calculated. You rang the supplier to query this and were told that your colleague, Graham Hyde, was aware of this and always agreed to the invoices before.

You suspect that your colleague is involved in fraud and possibly even money laundering but are not sure what best to do next.

(f) **Which of the following options describes what you should do next?** **(2 marks)**

Confront Graham with your suspicions	
Discuss the matter with Susan Wright, the chief accountant	
Call the police	
Resign	

Mike Ovey and Andrew Sach are worried whether there are other issues relating to the recording of purchases and amounts owed to suppliers. As a result of this, they ask you to perform a logic check of purchase ledger transactions for the month of September 20X6.

Using as many verified figures as possible, such as confirmed balances from suppliers, you construct the following purchase ledger control account:

Purchases ledger control account

	£		£
		Balance b/d	14,875
		Purchases day book	4,256
Contra	100		
Cash book	2,365		
Balance c/d	15,977		
Total		**Total**	

(g) **Calculate the missing figure in the purchases ledger control account.** **(1 mark)**

£ [   ]

(h) **Which of the following could the missing figure represent?** **(2 marks)**

Overstated purchase invoices	
Understated purchase invoices	

TASK 1.3 (15 marks)

This task is based on the workplace scenario of Ovey and Sach.

You are Tina Jeffrey, a part-qualified Accounting Technician. You work for Ovey and Sach, a business which makes and sells designer gifts. Ovey and Sach is a partnership owned by Mike Ovey and Andrew Sach.

You cover all aspects of bookkeeping and accounting for the business and report to Susan Wright, the chief accountant.

Today's date is 31 January 20X7.

Ovey and Sach are introducing a new product, the DFG. The budget is to sell 1,200 units 20X7 at an average selling price of £14. Incremental fixed production costs were budgeted to be £6,000 and the average variable production cost was expected to be £6 per unit.

(a)   Using the information above, determine the following budgeted figures for DFG for the year to 31 December 20X7, to the nearest whole number.   **(4 marks)**

	(i)	Break-even sales volume (units)	
	(ii)	Total break-even contribution (£)	
	(iii)	Total profit for the year (£)	
	(iv)	Margin of safety (units)	

Today's date is now 31 December 20X7.

The **actual** results for 20X7 were as follows:

- 1,200 units were made but only 1,100 units sold.

- The average variable production cost was £6.50 per unit.

- The average selling price was £13.45 per unit.

- Total fixed production costs were £6,240.

(b)   Calculate the following figures for the year to 31 December 20X7.   **(4 marks)**

	(i)	Closing inventory valued at actual marginal cost (£)	
	(ii)	Closing inventory valued at actual full cost (£)	
	(iii)	Profit if inventory is valued at actual marginal cost (£)	
	(iv)	Profit if inventory is valued at actual full cost (£)	

(c)   Write an email to Susan Wright in the fields below to report on the following points:

1   Three reasons for the difference between the budgeted and actual profit figures for 20X7.

2   The difference in profit between using marginal and absorption costing to value inventory.

3   Whether with absorption costing it would be ethical to boost production to close the profit shortfall.   **(6 marks)**

To: Susan Wright

From: Tina Jeffrey

Date: 31.12.X7

Subject: Performance of the new DFG product in 20X7

1

2

3

TASK 1.4 (15 marks)

This task is based on the workplace scenario of Ovey and Sach.

You are Tina Jeffrey, a part-qualified Accounting Technician. You work for Ovey and Sach, a business which makes and sells designer gifts. Ovey and Sach is a partnership owned by Mike Ovey and Andrew Sach.

You cover all aspects of bookkeeping and accounting for the business and report to Susan Wright, the chief accountant.

Today's date is 31 March 20X8.

Mike Ovey and Andrew Sach have decided to raise additional finance to increase the product range and grow the business. As part of a loan application they need to produce a report for the bank. Unfortunately Susan Wright is currently off sick and Andrew Sach has told you to produce the report.

The deadline suggested appears unrealistic, especially given the complexity of the work.

You feel that you are not sufficiently experienced to complete the work alone but your manager appears unable to offer the necessary support. You feel slightly intimidated by Andrew Sachs, and also feel under pressure to be a 'team player' and help out. However, if you try to complete the work to the required quality but fail, you could be subject to criticism and other repercussions.

(a) **Explain TWO threats to your ethical principles from Andrew Sach's request, and explain what actions you should take next. In your answer you should refer to the guidance found in the ethical code for professional accountants.** (6 marks)

Threat 1

```



```

Threat 2

```



```

Actions I should take

```



```

You receive the following email from Andrew Sach:

To: Tina Jeffrey

From: Andrew Sach

Date: 5/4/X8

Hello Tina

We have decided to delay completing the loan application until Susan is back with us as we feel it is vital that we get this right. Obviously we would still appreciate your input but want Susan to check everything before it goes to the bank.

In preliminary discussions with the bank I got the distinct impression that they would consider our application more favourably if we became a limited company rather than remain the partnership we currently operate as. I must confess to being confused and am now wondering whether we should be trying to raise new equity finance.

I would like you to tell me more about the implications of a partnership becoming a limited company as far as finance is concerned.

Please include three sections in your response to me as follows:

(1)   A brief description of a limited company and how switching could change the liability faced by Mike Ovey and myself.

(2)   Three reasons why the bank may prefer to lend to companies rather than partnerships.

(3)   The difference in the way companies can raise equity finance compared to a partnership.

Regards,
Andrew

(b)   Reply to Andrew, addressing all three points that he has raised.   (10 marks)

To:	Andrew Sachs
From:	Tina Jeffrey
Date:	5/4/X8

Subject:	

(1)	

(2)

(3)

PART 2

You will be required to open an **Excel spreadsheet** called **Laura** that contains data you require for this assessment. The spreadsheet can be found on MyKaplan. The spreadsheet will need to be downloaded and saved before starting the tasks.

You MUST save your work at regular intervals during this assessment to prevent you losing work.

TASK 2.1   (16 marks)

Laura's Luggage manufactures and sells luggage to retailers, online and through their own 'Factory' outlet.

The company wish to work out how well the '**Luxury**' brand of luggage has been performing in the online sales and have asked you to assist them by building a spreadsheet to help them calculate costs, revenue and profits for 20X4.

You have been asked to use the information below to prepare documents to show how the business has performed in the last twelve months.

Month	Opening inventory	Production volume	Sales volume
January	11,236	32,375	24,998
February		40,400	42,016
March		36,360	39,996
April		58,075	46,000
May		38,250	42,075
June		71,775	77,517
July		73,800	81,180
August		56,250	60,750
September		39,000	37,400
October		48,000	48,960
November		60,000	56,345
December		70,000	71,400

This data is given you in the sheet "volumes" in the Laura Workbook.

The table below shows the way in which the company calculated cost and sales prices during 20X4.

Quarter	Production cost	Sales price
Qtr 1	£48.50	Cost + 23%
Qtr 2	4%	Cost + 23%
Qtr 3	6%	Cost + 23%
Qtr 4	5%	Cost + 25%

(a)   Open a new workbook. Name the file as 'your surname, initial and assessment date (yyyymmdd)' and save the file. Insert a footer on every worksheet in the workbook with your full name and AAT student number in the left hand pane.

(b)   Open a new worksheet. Starting in Cell A5 input the monthly figures for opening inventory, production volumes and sales volumes in adjacent columns and create titles for the columns.

(c)   Insert a column after the sales volume column and call this closing inventory.

(d)   Use formulae to calculate the following:

•   The closing inventory for each month (closing inventory is calculated as opening Inventory plus production volume minus sales volume).

•   The opening inventory for each month by bringing forward the closing volume from the previous month.

•   The total production volumes for 20X4 and the total sales volume for 20X4.

(e)   Format the your table of data in the following way:

•   The figures in your table of data should be set to number to 0 decimal places with a 1000 separator.

•   The column headings, using bold, Arial, font size 11 and wrapped over 2 lines to reduce column width.

•   Totals should be in bold.

(f)   Insert the title 'Production and Sales Volumes 20X4', in the top row of your worksheet as bold, Arial and font size 14. The title should be merged and centred across the table of data and underlined.

(g)   In Row 23 you are going to create a second table of data that converts all the volumes from the table above into monetary figures.

1   Copy the column and row headings into the new table at Row 23.

2   Alter the column headings to Month, Opening Inventory, Variable Costs, Sales Revenue and Closing Inventory.

3   Use the table of quarterly production costs and sales prices (above) and convert the volumes to monetary values.

•   Closing inventory figures should still be brought forward.

•   Closing inventory should be valued at the production cost for the quarter.

•   The increase in production costs are a percentage increase from Quarter 1.

4   Total all the columns.

(h) You are now required to use formulae to calculate Gross and Net Profit figures. To do this you will need to do the following:

    1   Next to the closing inventory column create a column for Cost of Sales. As this is a manufacturing accounting-system, Cost of Sales is calculated as 'Opening Inventory plus Variable Costs minus closing inventory'.

    2   Alongside Cost of Sales create a column for Gross Profit. Gross Profit is calculated as 'Sales Revenue minus Cost of Sales.

    3   Alongside Gross Profit create a column for Expenses. Expenses are £63,000 in Quarter 1 rising by 5% in each successive quarter.

    4   Alongside Expenses create a column for Net Profit. Net Profit is calculated as 'Gross Profit minus Expenses'.

    5   Total all the columns.

(i) Alongside the Net Profit column create two more columns for Gross Profit Margin and Net Profit Margin.

    1   Gross Profit margin is Gross Profit as a percentage of Sales Revenue.

    2   Net Profit margin is Net Profit as a percentage of Sales Revenue.

    3   Calculate average Gross and Net Profit margins (average margins are calculated by expressing total gross/net profit as a percentage of total sales).

(j) Two rows above the table insert the title Profits and Margins for 20X4.

    1   The title should be in bold, underlined and Arial font size 14.

    2   The title should be merged and centred across all the columns.

(k) Format the table in the following way:

    1   Make sure that all the above columns are suitably labelled.

    2   Wrap text in the columns so that the columns are a suitable width.

    3   All column headers should be in **bold**.

    4   All column totals should be in **bold**.

    5   Format all monetary cells to currency to two decimal places.

    6   Percentages should be to two decimal places.

    7   Average margin figures should be **bold** and cell fill should be yellow.

    8   Name the worksheet Lugg001.

(l) Copy Lugg001 to a new worksheet and show formulas. Adjust column widths so the data fits neatly in the columns. Name this worksheet Lugg001(F).

(m) Prepare Lugg001 and Lugg001(F) so that they would print to 1 × A4 page if required. Choose the most suitable page orientation.

TASK 2.2 **(12 marks)**

You need to review the variable costs for the first quarter of 20X4 (January, February and March) which were entered onto the computer by your line manager. This information is in the Laura Workbook labelled as 'VCosts 20X4' in the Laura Workbook.

(a)   Unprotect the worksheet using VC20X4 as the password. Open a new worksheet in your workbook and copy only the relevant information from the 'VCosts20X4' worksheet. Replace the title with 'Variable Costs Quarter 1 20X4' using Arial font in size 14 in a merged cell (left aligned) over all the data columns. The title should be in bold, underlined and in Italics.

(b)   Format the column headers with bold text ensuring column widths and row heights are suitable for the contents. Wrap text across 2 lines.

(c)   Format all the dates as dd/mm/yyyy, make amendments as required so that all dates are in the required format. Sort the data by date, in ascending order, ensuring only the correct information is used for the quarter.

(d)   You have discovered additional Direct Materials and Variable Overheads not included in the spreadsheet. Insert rows and/or columns at the correct date and enter the following costs. Ensure the row total calculates correctly and it must remain as the last column on the worksheet.

• Direct Materials 7th February	£112,077.80
• Direct Materials 16 Jan 14	£179,440.10
• 5th Jan, Variable Overheads	£14,800
• 5th Feb, Variable Overheads	£12,300
• 5th March, Variable Overheads	£11,100

(e)   Total all the columns and then use functions to calculate the average and median Direct Material costs ensuring the cells containing the functions are clearly labelled. These labels should be in **bold**. Ensure the format of all numerical cells is currency rounded to two decimal places.

(f)   Use conditional formatting to highlight cells in which the Direct Materials values exceed the average figure for Direct Materials by 10%. The conditional formatting should change the cell fill to Red and the text to white and bold.

(g)   Produce a Pie Chart of the column totals. Insert the chart to the right of the variable costs data table. Ensure the legend contains the column header names and that the chart has a suitable title. The Pie Chart should show percentages.

(h)   Name this worksheet tab 'Quarter 1 VarCosts' and ensure all of the information is displayed in a way that could be printed on one A4 page. Save this worksheet.

TASK 2.3 (12 marks)

Laura's Luggage sells a range of ladies bags. All sales have been recorded on the 'LLData' worksheet in the Laura Workbook. Copy the data from this worksheet into a new worksheet in your workbook.

You have been asked to identify the most popular type of bag sold and the best performing sales method, (Internet, Factory Shop or Retail) from this information of each type of sale.

You need to create pivot table(s) from this information to identify the most popular ladies bag by value and the value of the sales for each outlet.

(a)   Check the data table to ensure there is nothing to prevent pivot tables from working. Make any changes you feel necessary to update the table (do not alter any values).

(b)   There has been an error in inputting; Internet sales have been recorded both as 'Internet' and 'Online'. Replace all instances of 'Online' with 'Internet'.

(c)   Create a pivot table with an appropriate heading. The pivot table should be placed to the right of the data set. Use the pivot table to identify the most popular type of bag sold by value and sales outlet. Identify the bag that generates the highest income by colouring the font of the highest income figures red.

(d)   Create another pivot table with an appropriate heading to show total sales by sales outlet (Internet, Factory Shop or Retail), indicating which one of the three outlets generates the most income. You may need to update the data in some way to allow this to be done.

(e)   Colour the font of the highest income figure red and arrange the figures of the pivot table in descending order. Name the tab 'Bags' and remember to save your work.

Section 6

MOCK ASSESSMENT – ANSWERS

PART 1

TASK 1.1   (15 marks)

(a)   **Are these statements true or false?**   (2 marks)

Statement	True	False
The AAT code of ethics gives detailed rules that cover a wide range of possible scenarios.		x
Some of the ethical principles can be overlooked if it is in the public interest to do so.	x	

Note:

1   The code gives principles rather than rules.

2   An example of this would be whistleblowing, where confidentiality is breached.

(b)   **For each of the following scenarios identify the nature of the ethical threat.**   (2 marks)

Scenario	Threat
Siobahn is seconded to internal audit and asked to verify that control procedures have been followed correctly, including bank reconciliations.	Self-review threat
Siobahn's brother is one of Plug Ltd's suppliers.	Familiarity threat

(c)   **Identify whether the following statements are true or false.**   (3 marks)

Statement	True	False
Siobahn may never disclose confidential information to any third party.		x
The threat that Siobahn is facing to her compliance with the fundamental principles is a self-interest threat.		x
Siobahn must resign immediately from Plug Ltd as her integrity has been compromised by her past relationships.		x

Note:

1   Siobahn may disclose information if given permission to do so.

2   This is an example of an intimidation threat.

3   Siobahn should discuss the matter with her manager and possibly even with the police.

(d) **Complete the following statement.** **(2 marks)**

Being offered gifts by the rival firm is | a self-interest threat | to Terry's fundamental

principle of | objectivity |

(e) **Identify whether the following statements are true or false.** **(3 marks)**

Statement	True	False
Had he accepted the holiday, Terry would have been guilty of the offence of 'active' bribery under the UK Bribery Act (2010).		x
The UK Bribery Act (2010) only applies to UK citizens, residents and companies established under UK law.		x
Not all gifts or hospitality would be considered to be bribes.	x	

Note:

1   Terry would have been guilty of "passive" bribery – receiving a bribe.

2   The UK Act also applies to.

3   Very small gifts or acts of hospitality would not be considered bribes.

(f) **Identify whether the following statements are true or false.** **(3 marks)**

Statement	True	False
Terry should report the matter to the firm's MRLO.	x	
Plug Ltd should scrutinise the request carefully before agreeing to any payment.	x	
Unless investigations satisfy any concerns raised, then the MRLO should fill in a Suspicious Activity Report (SAR) to be sent to the NCA.	x	

Note:

There is a strong suspicion of money laundering in these circumstances.

TASK 1.2 (16 marks)

(a) **At the end of which month does Ovey and Sach Ltd exceed the registration threshold?**

(2 marks)

February 20X6	
March 20X6	x
April 20X6	
December 20X6	

The historic registration test is based on a business exceeding £83,000 of taxable turnover in the last 12 months or since starting in business if this is less than 12 months. Taxable turnover excludes exempt supplies but includes zero-rated supplies.

Working: Cumulative taxable turnover for the last 12 months

		£
End Dec 20X5	(£6,000 × 12)	72,000
End Jan 20X6	(£72,000 + £5,600 Jan X6 – £6,000 Jan X5))	71,600
End Feb 20X6	(£71,600 + £11,100 Feb X6 – £6,000 Feb X5)	76,700
End Mar 20X6	(£76,700 + £13,100 Mar X6 – £6,000 Mar X5)	83,800

(b) **Identify which of the following reasons might explain why a business would NOT voluntarily register for VAT?** (4 marks)

Statement	True	False
It makes their goods more expensive for other VAT-registered businesses.		x
It makes their goods more expensive for businesses that are not VAT-registered.	x	
It helps to avoid penalties for late registration.		x
It increases the business burden of administration.	x	

(c) **What is the tax point date?** (2 marks)

4 May 20X6	
15 May 20X6	
20 May 20X6	x
28 June 20X6	

Note:

The basic tax point is the date of delivery of goods or the date of performance of services. Where goods are not paid for or invoiced in advance, a later tax point can arise if a tax invoice is raised within 14 days after the basic tax point. The basic tax point date is 15 May (i.e. date the goods are delivered). However, the actual tax point date is the invoice date as the valid invoice is issued and sent on 20 May (i.e. within 14 days of 15 May).

(d) **What figure will be inserted in Box 1 of the VAT return for the VAT period ended 30 September 20X6?** **(1 mark)**

£	4,801.63

Box 1 of the VAT return = VAT due on sales and other outputs.

5,587.32 – 785.69 = 4,801.63

(e) **Once the journals have been processed, what will be the revised balance carried down on the VAT account?** **(2 marks)**

£	5,177.58

Input VAT should be £56.50 higher, so the balance should be 5,234.08 – 56.50.

The zero rated sales invoice will not affect the VAT balance.

(f) **Which of the following options describes what you should do next?** **(2 marks)**

Confront Graham with your suspicions	
Discuss the matter with Susan Wright, the chief accountant	x
Call the police	
Resign	

(g) **Calculate the missing figure in the purchases ledger control account.** **(1 mark)**

£	689

Purchases ledger control account

	£		£
		Balance b/d	14,875
		Purchases day book	4,256
Contra	100		
Cash book	2,365		
Balance c/d	15,977		
Difference	689		
Total	19,131	**Total**	19,131

(h) **Which of the following could the missing figure represent?** **(2 marks)**

Overstated purchase invoices	x
Understated purchase invoices	

Given the difference is on the debit side, then one cause could be the credit side being too high – the PDB figure is overstated.

TASK 1.3 (15 marks)

(a) **Determine the following budgeted figures for DFG for the year to 31 December 20X7, to the nearest whole number.** (4 marks)

(i) Break-even sales volume	750
(ii) Total break-even contribution	6,000
(iii) Total profit for the year	3,600
(iv) Margin of safety	450

(b) **Calculate the actual profit for the year to 31 December 20X7 under the following scenarios.** (4 marks)

(i) Closing inventory valued at actual marginal cost (£)	650
(ii) Closing inventory valued at actual full cost (£)	1,170
(iii) Profit if inventory is valued at actual marginal cost (£)	1,405
(iv) Profit if inventory is valued at actual full cost (£)	1,925

Workings:

Value of closing inventory per unit (MC) = 6.50

Total value of closing inventory (MC) = 100 × 6.50 = £650

Value of closing inventory per unit (TAC) = 6.50 + (6,240/1,200) = 6.50 + 5.20 = 11.70

Total value of closing inventory (TAC) = 100 × 11.70 = £1,170

Profit using MC = 1,100 × (13.45 – 6.50) – 6,240 = £1,405

Profit using TAC = 1,100 × (13.45 – 11.70) = £1,925

(c) To: Susan Wright

From: Tina Jeffrey

Date: 31.12.X7

Subject: Performance of the new DFG product in 20X7

1	Actual profit was lower than budgeted.
	This was due to the following factors:
	(1) Sales volumes were only 1,100 units rather than the 1,200 budgeted.
	(2) Fixed costs were £240 higher than expected at £6,240 compared to £6,000.
	(3) The average variable production cost was £0.50 per unit higher at £6.50 per unit, compared to the £6 per unit budgeted.

2	Inventory valuation.
	Closing inventory is valued at £1,170 under absorption costing and £650 under marginal costing. The absorption costing valuation is £520 higher due to fixed production overheads being absorbed.
	This £520 higher valuation has resulted in profit being £520 higher under absorption costing (£1,925) compared to marginal costing (£1,405).

3	Ethical concern.
	Under absorption costing increasing production without increasing sales will boost profit and hence close some of the profit shortfall.
	Whether this is unethical depends on whether or not the extra inventory can be sold, say if sales in 20X8 are expected to grow further.
	If, however, the additional inventory would end up being thrown away due to obsolescence or deterioration, then it would be unethical to make additional units just to hit profit targets.

TASK 1.4 (15 marks)

(a)   Threat 1

> **Professional competence and due care:**
>
> It would not be right for me to attempt to complete work that is technically beyond my abilities without proper supervision.
>
> This is made worse by my concern whether it is even possible to complete the work within the time available and still act diligently to achieve the required quality of output.

Threat 2

> **Objectivity:**
>
> Pressure from Andrew Sach, combined with the fear of repercussions, gives rise to an intimidation threat to my objectivity.
>
> If the loan application is unsuccessful then there is also the possibility that will impact other people's jobs, again adding to threat to objectivity.

Actions I should take

> I should use the Conceptual Framework to apply relevant safeguards to bring the threat to my principles down to an acceptable level OR I should use the ethical conflict resolution process stated in the code. I should follow any internal procedure for reporting/dealing with such threats.
>
> I should discuss my concerns with Andrew Sachs that I do not have sufficient time and experience to complete the work to a satisfactory standard and suggest how the problem may be resolved. For example, the use of a subcontract accountant or the possibility of assigning another member of staff to supervise my work.
>
> If I am still under pressure to do the work, then I should get advice from the AAT and as to what to do next.
>
> It would be unethical to attempt to complete the work if I doubt my competence.

(b) **Reply to Andrew, addressing all three points that he has raised.** **(10 marks)**

To:	Andrew Sachs
From:	Tina Jeffrey
Date:	5/4/X8

Subject:	Raising finance

(1) | **Limited companies**

A limited company is an organisation that is a separate legal entity distinct from its owners (unlike a partnership or sole trader). The ownership of a company is through share ownership.

At present Mike Ovey and yourself have unlimited personal liability for partnership debts. With a "limited" company the liability of owners (shareholders) is limited to any unpaid amounts on shares purchased. Thus, for example, the bank would not be able to pursue Mike Ovey and yourself if the business struggled to repay the loan.

For this reason, some banks may insist on personal guarantees from the owners, separate from the company.

(2) | **Bank loans**

Banks may prefer to lend to companies for the following reasons:

(1) A limited company must prepare annual accounts (also known as 'statutory accounts') from the company's records at the end of the financial year. Partners are not legally required to produce annual accounts or file accounts for inspection.

(2) Larger companies' financial statements must be audited, possibly making them more reliable and accurate.

(3) A company's accounts must be prepared in accordance with the Companies Act 2006, possibly making it easier to assess the business' performance.

(3) | **Equity finance**

Companies can raise equity finance by issuing new shares to investors.

With partnerships, either the existing partners could introduce further capital or a new partner could be admitted. Introducing new partners would involve having to change the partnership agreement.

PART 2

TASK 2.1

Production and Sales Volumes 20X4			
Month	Opening Inventory	Production volume	Sales Volume	Closing inventory
January	11,236	32,375	24,998	18,613
February	18,613	40,400	42,016	16,997
March	16,997	36,360	39,996	13,361
April	13,361	58,075	46,000	25,436
May	25,436	38,250	42,075	21,611
June	21,611	71,775	77,517	15,869
July	15,869	73,800	81,180	8,489
August	8,489	56,250	60,750	3,989
September	3,989	39,000	37,400	5,589
October	5,589	48,000	48,960	4,629
November	4,629	60,000	56,345	8,284
December	8,284	70,000	71,400	6,884
		624,285	628,637	

Month	Opening Inventory	Production volume	Sales Volume	Closing inventory
January	11236	32375	24998	=B5+C5-D5
February	=E5	40400	42016	=B6+C6-D6
March	=E6	36360	39996	=B7+C7-D7
April	=E7	58075	46000	=B8+C8-D8
May	=E8	38250	42075	=B9+C9-D9
June	=E9	71775	77517	=B10+C10-D10
July	=E10	73800	81180	=B11+C11-D11
August	=E11	56250	60750	=B12+C12-D12
September	=E12	39000	37400	=B13+C13-D13
October	=E13	48000	48960	=B14+C14-D14
November	=E14	60000	56345	=B15+C15-D15
December	=E15	70000	71400	=B16+C16-D16
		=SUM(C5:C16)	=SUM(D5:D16)	

Profits and Margins for 20X4

Month	Opening Inventory	Variable Costs	Sales Revenue	Closing Inventory	Cost of Sales	Gross Profit	Expenses	Net Profit	Gross Profit Margin	Net Profit Margin
January	£544,946.00	£1,570,187.50	£1,491,380.68	£902,730.50	£1,212,403.00	£278,977.68	£63,000.00	£215,977.68	18.71%	14.48%
February	£902,730.50	£1,959,400.00	£2,506,674.56	£824,354.50	£2,037,776.00	£468,898.56	£63,000.00	£405,898.56	18.71%	16.19%
March	£824,354.50	£1,763,460.00	£2,386,161.36	£648,008.50	£1,939,806.00	£446,355.36	£63,000.00	£383,355.36	18.71%	16.07%
April	£648,008.50	£2,929,303.00	£2,853,840.00	£1,282,991.84	£2,294,319.66	£559,520.34	£66,150.00	£493,370.34	19.61%	17.29%
May	£1,282,991.84	£1,929,330.00	£2,610,333.00	£1,090,058.84	£2,122,263.00	£488,070.00	£66,150.00	£421,920.00	18.70%	16.16%
June	£1,090,058.84	£3,620,331.00	£4,809,154.68	£800,432.36	£3,909,957.48	£899,197.20	£66,150.00	£833,047.20	18.70%	17.32%
July	£800,432.36	£3,794,058.00	£5,133,011.40	£436,419.49	£4,158,070.87	£974,940.53	£69,457.50	£905,483.03	18.99%	17.64%
August	£436,419.49	£2,891,812.50	£3,841,222.50	£205,074.49	£3,123,157.50	£718,065.00	£69,457.50	£648,607.50	18.69%	16.89%
September	£205,074.49	£2,004,990.00	£2,364,802.00	£287,330.49	£1,922,734.00	£442,068.00	£69,457.50	£372,610.50	18.69%	15.76%
October	£287,330.49	£2,444,640.00	£3,116,793.60	£235,754.97	£2,496,215.52	£620,578.08	£72,930.38	£547,647.71	19.91%	17.57%
November	£235,754.97	£3,055,800.00	£3,586,922.70	£421,904.12	£2,869,650.85	£717,271.85	£72,930.38	£644,341.48	20.00%	17.96%
December	£421,904.12	£3,565,100.00	£4,545,324.00	£350,602.12	£3,636,402.00	£908,922.00	£72,930.38	£835,991.63	20.00%	18.39%
	£7,680,006.10	£31,528,412.00	£39,245,620.48	£7,485,662.22	£31,722,755.88	£7,522,864.60	£814,613.63	£6,708,250.98	19.17%	17.09%

This table has been included here to show where the numbers have come from for the calculation of variable costs, sales revenue and closing inventory.

Quarter	Production Cost	Sales Price
Qtr 1	£48.50	£59.66
Qtr 2	£50.44	£62.04
Qtr 3	£51.41	£63.23
Qtr 4	£50.93	£63.66

Profits and Margins for 20X4

Month	Opening Inventory	Variable Costs	Sales Revenue	Closing inventory	Cost of Sales	Gross Profit	Expenses	Net Profit	Gross Profit Margin	Net Profit Margin
January	=B5*48.5	=C5*48.5	=D5*59.66	=E5*48.5	=B24+C24-E24	=D24-F24	63000	=G24-H24	=G24/D24	=I24/D24
February	=E24	=C6*48.5	=D6*59.66	=E6*48.5	=B25+C25-E25	=D25-F25	63000	=G25-H25	=G25/D25	=I25/D25
March	=E25	=C7*48.5	=D7*59.66	=E7*48.5	=B26+C26-E26	=D26-F26	63000	=G26-H26	=G26/D26	=I26/D26
April	=E26	=C8*50.44	=D8*62.04	=E8*50.44	=B27+C27-E27	=D27-F27	=$H$26*1.05	=G27-H27	=G27/D27	=I27/D27
May	=E27	=C9*50.44	=D9*62.04	=E9*50.44	=B28+C28-E28	=D28-F28	=$H$26*1.05	=G28-H28	=G28/D28	=I28/D28
June	=E28	=C10*50.44	=D10*62.04	=E10*50.44	=B29+C29-E29	=D29-F29	=$H$26*1.05	=G29-H29	=G29/D29	=I29/D29
July	=E29	=C11*51.41	=D11*63.23	=E11*51.41	=B30+C30-E30	=D30-F30	=$H$29*1.05	=G30-H30	=G30/D30	=I30/D30
August	=E30	=C12*51.41	=D12*63.23	=E12*51.41	=B31+C31-E31	=D31-F31	=$H$29*1.05	=G31-H31	=G31/D31	=I31/D31
September	=E31	=C13*51.41	=D13*63.23	=E13*51.41	=B32+C32-E32	=D32-F32	=$H$29*1.05	=G32-H32	=G32/D32	=I32/D32
October	=E32	=C14*50.93	=D14*63.66	=E14*50.93	=B33+C33-E33	=D33-F33	=$H$32*1.05	=G33-H33	=G33/D33	=I33/D33
November	=E33	=C15*50.93	=D15*63.66	=E15*50.93	=B34+C34-E34	=D34-F34	=$H$32*1.05	=G34-H34	=G34/D34	=I34/D34
December	=E34	=C16*50.93	=D16*63.66	=E16*50.93	=B35+C35-E35	=D35-F35	=$H$32*1.05	=G35-H35	=G35/D35	=I35/D35
	=SUM(B24:B35)	=SUM(C24:C35)	=SUM(D24:D35)	=SUM(E24:E35)	=SUM(F24:F35)	=SUM(G24:G35)	=SUM(H24:H35)	=SUM(I24:I35)	=G36/D36	=I36/D36

Quarter	Production Cost	Sales Price
Qtr 1	48.5	=B39*1.23
Qtr 2	=B39*1.04	=B40*1.23
Qtr 3	=B39*1.06	=B41*1.23
Qtr 4	=B39*1.05	=B42*1.25

This table has been included here to show where the numbers have come from for the calculation of variable costs, sales revenue and closing inventory. You refer to the cells in the formula bu you would need to remember to use 'absolute' referencing where appropriate.

TASK 2.2

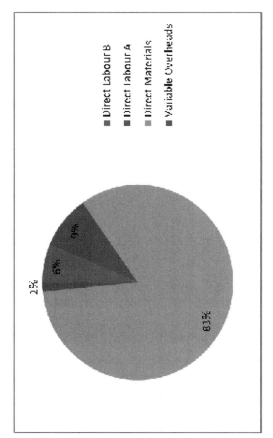

Variable Costs Quarter 1 20X4

Date	Direct Labour B	Direct Labour A	Direct Materials	Variable Overheads	Total
02/01/2014			£172,538.60		£172,538.60
05/01/2014			£95,804.56	£14,800.00	£110,604.56
09/01/2014			£92,119.77		£92,119.77
12/01/2014			£147,486.72		£147,486.72
16/01/2014			£99,636.74		£99,636.74
16/01/2014			£121,223.33		£121,223.33
16/01/2014			£179,440.10		£179,440.10
30/01/2014	£39,822.92	£56,548.54			£96,371.45
05/02/2014			£126,072.27	£12,300.00	£138,372.27
06/02/2014			£78,036.98		£78,036.98
07/02/2014			£112,077.80		£112,077.80
11/02/2014			£103,622.21		£103,622.21
27/02/2014	£45,201.42	£64,186.02			£109,387.44
27/02/2014			£81,189.68		£81,189.68
05/03/2014				£11,100.00	£11,100.00
06/03/2014			£131,115.16		£131,115.16
08/03/2014			£107,767.10		£107,767.10
12/03/2014			£88,576.70		£88,576.70
14/03/2014			£159,521.64		£159,521.64
14/03/2014			£79,597.72		£79,597.72
15/03/2014			£136,359.76		£136,359.76
30/03/2014	£73,736.19	£104,705.39			£178,441.58
	£158,760.53	£225,439.95	£2,112,186.87	£38,200.00	£2,534,587.34
Average			£117,343.71		
Median			£109,922.45		

If your costs don't match make sure you have only included Jan to Mar in the table as we only want the details for the first quarter.

TASK 2.3

	A	B	C	D	E
1	Sales Outlet	Handbags	Clutch Bags	Shoulder Bags	Total
2	Internet	330	268	948	1546
3	Factory Shop	258	785	630	1673
4	Factory Shop	258	268	967	1493
5	Internet	316	780	967	2063
6	Internet	794	1019	989	2802
7	Retail	258	740	954	1952
8	Factory Shop	938	458	514	1910
9	Internet	698	601	357	1656
10	Factory Shop	842	601	620	2063
11	Retail	623	867	514	2004
12	Factory Shop	867	536	832	2235
13	Internet	757	979	258	1994
14	Factory Shop	393	600	635	1628
15	Retail	391	432	868	1691
16	Factory Shop	758	961	879	2598
17	Internet	879	797	512	2188
18	Retail	698	960	381	2039
19	Internet	498	1036	280	1814
20	Factory Shop	380	380	745	1505
21	Internet	979	1092	740	2811
22	Factory Shop	258	82	502	842
23	Retail	380	258	907	1545
24	Internet	380	960	270	1610
25	Factory Shop	366	499	380	1245
26	Internet	598	1380	895	2873
27	Factory Shop	313	108	501	922

Income by bag type

	Values		
Sales Outlet ▼	Sum o Sum of Clutch Bags		Sum of Shoulder Bags
Factory Shop	5631	5278	7205
Internet	6229	8912	6216
Retail	2350	3257	3624
Grand Total	**14210**	**17447**	**17045**

Income by outlet

Sum of Total	
Sales Outlet ↓	Total
Internet	21357
Factory Shop	18114
Retail	9231
Grand Total	**48702**

Section 7

SAMPLE ASSESSMENT 2 – QUESTIONS

PART 1

TASK 1.1 **(15 marks)**

This task is based on a workplace scenario separate to the rest of the assessment.

Accountant, Wajid, has recently started work at Hook Ltd, a large organisation with many employees. He is trying to apply the ethical code's conceptual framework to an ethical problem he ~~is facing~~ at work. He is currently evaluating threats to his fundamental principles.

(a) **Complete the following statement** **(2 marks)**

To resolve the matter the conceptual framework states that Wajid must use...

∇

∇ Drop down list for task 1.1 (a)

the advice of a lawyer.
his professional judgement.
his common sense.

(b) **For each of the following examples identify whether there is a conflict to be resolved between the behaviour of Hook Ltd's management and Sherie's personal values.**

(2 marks)

Example of behaviour of Hook Ltd's management	Sherie's personal value	Is there a conflict to resolve?
Long-standing employees are allowed an extra half day's holiday for every two years to permanent employment with Hook Ltd	Loyalty	∇
Employees are promoted on the basis of family or other close relationships	Fairness	∇

∇ Drop down list for task 1.1 (b)

Yes
No

A potential customer of Hook Ltd has asked Sherie to reveal confidential information about Hook Ltd's cost structure and pricing strategy. The potential customer has offered to pay Sherie for this information.

(c)   **Identify whether the following statements are true or false**   **(3 marks)**

Statement	True	False
Sherie may never disclose confidential information to any third party.		
The threat that Sherie is facing to her compliance with the fundamental principles is a self-interest threat.		
Sherie must resign immediately from Hook Ltd as her integrity has been compromised by the offer from the potential customer.		

Ian is also an accountant with Hook Ltd. The manager of one of Hook Ltd's main suppliers has offered Ian gifts. Ian has known the manager for several years.

(d)   **Complete the following statement**   **(2 mark**

Being offered gifts by the manager is [＿＿＿＿＿ ∇] to Ian's fundamental

principle of [＿＿＿＿＿ ∇]

∇ Drop down list for task 1.1 (d)

an intimidation threat
a familiarity threat
objectivity.
professional competence and due care.

Ian is following the conflict resolution process in the ethical code in respect of an ethical dilemma at work. Ian has collected evidence and documented the process carefully so he can seek guidance on the dilemma from his friend Antoine, an accountant who works for another organisation.

(e)   **Complete the following statement**   **(2 marks)**

In relation to the evidence and documentation, Ian must be particularly careful to

ensure the fundamental principle of [＿＿＿＿＿ ∇] Is not

breached when seeking guidance from Antoine.

∇ Drop down list for task 1.1 (e)

confidentiality
professional competence and due care
professional behaviour

Ellie is an accountant who works for a professional accountancy firm. She has a client who has been involved in concealing criminal property. Ellie has reported the client to the relevant authority, and has told the client about this.

(f)   Complete the following statement   **(2 marks)**

Ellie has committed the criminal offence of

	∇

∇ Drop down list for task 1.1 (f)

money laundering
failure to disclose
tipping off

Luke is an accountant in practice, working as a sole practitioner. He has discovered that a client has been money laundering.

(g)   Complete the following statement   **(2 marks)**

Luke should disclose confidential information on this matter directly to

	∇

∇ Drop down list for task 1.1 (g)

The Money Laundering Reporting Officer.
The National Crime Agency.
HMRC.

TASK 1.2   **(16 marks)**

This task is based on the workplace scenario of NewPlace.

You are Chris Makepeace, a part-qualified Accounting Technician. You work for NewPlace, a business which retails office equipment. NewPlace is owned and run by Mo Hussain.

You cover all aspects of bookkeeping and accounting for the business. NewPlace also uses the services of Addo & Co, a firm of accountants. Kiera Jackson is the accountant at Addo & Co who carries out tasks for NewPlace.

Today's date is 15 April 20X7. You are checking the non-current assets register. A vehicle acquired on 1 January was recorded as a van at £10,000 cost. You find the related purchased invoice.

To: NewPlace 200-210 Farm Road Endsleigh EN1 7DS	From: Car Sales Ltd 178 Judd Road Endsleigh EN62 8SP	Date and tax point: 01 January 20X7 Invoice CJL 69840 VAT 132 5895 01 GB
		£
1.6 litre car VY12 ALK	Purchase Order 584	10,000.00
	VAT at 20%	2,000.00
	Total	12,000.00
Delivery date: 01/01/X7		

You establish that

- the vehicle is a company car for the sales manager's private and business use

- in the ledger accounts the purchase was entered as:

Account	Debit £	Credit £
Vehicles at cost	10,000.00	
VAT	2,000.00	
Bank		12,000.00

- input tax was reclaimed in the VAT return to 31 March 20X7

- VAT on the purchase of the car should not be reclaimed as input tax.

(a) **Show the entries that need to be made in the general ledger to correct the £2,000 VAT that was reclaimed.**

Make each selection by clicking on a box in the left column and then on one in the right column. You can remove a line by clicking on it. **(2 marks)**

Account
Bank
Depreciation charges
Disposals of non-current assets
Suspense
VAT
Vehicles accumulated depreciation
Vehicles at cost
Vehicles running expenses

Debit £2,000.00
Credit £2,000.00

You tell Mo that reclaiming VAT on the car is not allowed under the VAT regulations. Mo tells you that Addo & Co stated that input VAT can be reclaimed on vans but not cars. He therefore decided to treat the car as a van to achieve a reclaim on the VAT.

(b) **Complete each of the following statements to show the action you advise.** **(4 marks)**

I advise that the VAT reclaim is an error that...

...can be ignored.	
...must be reported separately to HMRC.	
...can be corrected on the current VAT return without a separate report to HMRC.	

This action should be taken because...

...the error was deliberate.	
...of the size of the error.	
...Mo made a mistake that was reasonable in the circumstances.	

No action has been taken to change the VAT treatment either in the accounts or with HMRC. You consider consulting a technical helpline set up by your local college to determine what you should do next.

(c) **According to the ethical code, which of your fundamental principles would be under threat if you called the helpline?** **(1 mark)**

Objectivity	
Confidentiality	

You decide not to consult the technical helpline so you must now consider your position with regards to the ethical code.

(d) **Do you need to take further action to ensure your compliance with the ethical code in this case?** **(2 marks)**

No, no further action by me is necessary because it is Mo's responsibility to decide how to proceed.	
Yes, I should inform Mo in writing that my professional principles prevent me from being connected with the VAT return or other related information submitted to HMRC.	
Yes, I am obliged to inform HMRC about the error myself.	

In relation to the VAT reclaim on the company car, Mo has now agreed to take the appropriate action both in the ledger accounts and with respect to HMRC.

You are recording the annual depreciation charge for the new car. Vehicles are depreciated at 25% per year on a diminishing balance basis.

(e) **Answer to following:**

(i) **Prepare the journal for the first full year's depreciation on the car based on its corrected cost in the general ledger.** **(4 marks)**

Journal

	Dr £	Cr £
▽		
▽		

∇ Drop down list for task 1.2 (e) (i)

Administration expenses
Bank
Depreciation charges
Disposals of non-current assets
Purchases
Purchases ledger control account
Sales
Sales ledger control account
Suspense
VAT
Vehicle running expenses
Vehicles accumulated depreciation
Vehicles at costs
<empty>

(ii) **Complete the following statement about the overall effect on the business's profit for the year of correcting the VAT reclaim.** **(1 mark)**

NewPlace's profit for the year will be [∇] than if the VAT reclaim had not been corrected

∇ Drop down list for task 1.2 (e) (ii)

higher
lower

Kiera Jackson at Addo & Co finds out about Mo's attempt to reclaim VAT incorrectly. Kiera believes she has reason to suspect that this was part of a money laundering operation at NewPlace.

(f) **What should Kiera do next?** **(2 marks)**

Discuss the matter in full with Mo.	
Make a Suspicious Activity Report to the relevant external authority, detailing her suspicions.	
Make an internal report within Addo & Co detailing her suspicions.	

TASK 1.3 (15 marks)

This task is based on the workplace scenario of NewPlace.

You are Chris Makepeace, a part-qualified Accounting Technician. You work for NewPlace, a business which retails office equipment. NewPlace is owned and run by Mo Hussain.

You cover all aspects of bookkeeping and accounting for the business. NewPlace also uses the services of Addo & Co, a firm of accountants. Kiera Jackson is the accountant at Addo & Co who carries out tasks for NewPlace.

Today's date is 31 January 20X8. In December 20X6 NewPlace produced a budget for its sales revenue, costs, and profit for the year to 31 December 20X7.

The budget was to sell 20,000 units of office equipment in 20X7. Fixed costs were budgeted to be £600,000 and the average sales price per unit was expected to be £170. The average unit cost was expected to be £120.

(a) **Using the information above, determine the following budgeted figures for the year to 31 December 20X7, to the nearest whole number.** (4 marks)

(i)	Break-even sales volume		units
(ii)	Total break-even contribution	£	
(iii)	Total profit for the year	£	
(iv)	Margin of safety		units

The following are extracts from NewPlace's trial balance at 31 December 20X7.

Account	Debit £	Credit £
Non-current assets accumulated depreciation		450,000
Administration overheads	120,000	
Depreciation on non-current assets for the year	150,000	
Direct materials (cost of items sold)	2,340,000	
Direct labour (wages of store staff)	180,000	
Rent and rates overheads	168,000	
Non-current assets at cost	920,000	
Purchases ledger control		170,000
Sales revenue		3,200,000
Sales ledger control	400,000	

20,000 units (items of office equipment) were actually made and sold during the year. There were no semi-variable costs.

(b) **Using the information from the trial balance, calculate the following actual figures for the year to 31 December 20X7.** (4 marks)

(i)	Total variable cost	£	
(ii)	Total fixed cost	£	
(iii)	Total contribution	£	
(iv)	Profit for the year	£	

(c)   **Write an email to Mo Hussain in the fields below to report on the following points:**

   1   **the difference between the budgeted and actual profit figures for 20X7**

   2   **the break-even volume based on the actual figures for 20X7 (show your workings)**

   3   **the reasons why the actual break-even point for 20X7 was different from the budgeted break-even point.**   **(6 marks)**

To: Mo Hussain Mo.Hussaine@NewPlace.co.uk

From: Chris Makepeace Chris.Makepeace@NewPlace.co.uk

Date: 31.1.X8

Subject: Performance of NewPlace for 20X7

1

2

3

TASK 1.4   **(15 marks)**

This task is based on the workplace scenario of NewPlace.

You are Chris Makepeace, a part-qualified Accounting Technician. You work for NewPlace, a business which retails office equipment. NewPlace is owned and run by Mo Hussain.

You cover all aspects of bookkeeping and accounting for the business. NewPlace also uses the services of Addo & Co, a firm of accountants. Kiera Jackson is the accountant at Addo & Co who carries out tasks for NewPlace.

Today's date is 28 February 20X8.

You help to record invoices from NewPlace's suppliers and also to make payments to them. You are aware that all phone calls on the NewPlace office phone are recorded.

For many years, DJ Furniture (DJ) has supplied NewPlace with items to sell in its stores, Janey Greene, the financial director at DJ, has telephoned your office several times during February. She has repeatedly asked you when certain large invoices will be paid, as DJ has cash flow difficulties. Each time you have replied that all invoices will be paid when they become due, in line with NewPlace procedures.

On 21 February you received a call on your private mobile phone from Janey. She invited you and your partner to attend an expensive Premier League football match with her and other DJ directors. You said you weren't sure if you could attend, and ended the phone call.

On 27 February you received another mobile call from Janey, demanding that you organise immediate payment of an invoice even though it had not become due. During the call, Janey said that if you refused to make the payment she would tell Mo that you demanded Premier League tickets from her in return for making early payments.

(a) **Explain TWO threats to your ethical principles from Janey's actions, and explain what actions you should take next. In your answer you should refer to the guidance found in the ethical code for professional accountants.** **(5 marks)**

Threat 1

___

Threat 2

___

Actions I should take

___

You receive the following email from Mo Hussain:

To: Chris Makepeace Chris.Makepeace@NewPlace.co.uk

From: Mo Hussain Mo.Hussaine@NewPlace.co.uk

Date: 28/2/X8

Hello Chris

I know you have nearly finalised the statement of profit or loss and the statement of financial position for NewPlace for the year ended 31 December 20X7. I would like to know more about the accounting principles they are based on, and how the two statements link together. Also, an accountant friend of mine was telling me about the fundamental qualitative characteristics of useful financial information the other day, but I couldn't really understand what she said.

I would like you to do the following:

(1)   Describe the TWO key assumptions that underlie the preparation of financial statements, using a relevant example in each case.

(2)   Describe ONE of the two fundamental qualitative characteristics of useful financial information.

(3)   Explain what the statement of financial position tells me.

(4)   Explain ONE way in which the statement of financial position links with the statement of profit or loss.

As I am not an accountant, I would be grateful if you could communicate your responses in a clear manner.

Regards,
Mo

(b)   Reply to Mo, addressing all four points that he has raised.   **(10 marks)**

To:	Mo Hussain Mo.Hussaine@NewPlace.co.uk
From:	Chris Makepeace Chris.Makepeace@NewPlace.co.uk
Date:	28/2/X8

Subject:	
(1)	
(2)	

PART 2

TASK 2.1 (10 marks)

Download the spreadsheet file from the assessment environment. Save the spreadsheet file in the appropriate location and rename it in the following format: 'your initial-surname-AAT no-dd.mm.yy-Task2.1'.

For example: J-Donnovan-123456-12.03.xx-Task2.1

A high degree of accuracy is required. You must save your work as an .XLS or .XLSX file at regular intervals to avoid losing your work.

You are Chris Makepeace, a part-qualified Accounting Technician. You work for NewPlace, a business which retails office equipment. NewPlace is owned and run by Mo Hussain.

You cover all aspects of bookkeeping and accounting for the business. NewPlace also uses the services of Addo & Co, a firm of accountants. Kiera Jackson is the accountant at Addo & Co who carries out tasks for NewPlace.

Today's date is 28 March 20X8.

NewPlace holds inventory of office equipment at its three separate stores. Identical product lists have been used to perform a stock take at each store. The results are shown in the worksheets labelled 'Store 1', 'Store 2' and 'Store 3'. Mo Hussain wants to identify high value items in inventory and also the value of the inventory that NewPlace holds from non-furniture suppliers (NFS).

(a) Open your renamed spreadsheet file. In the worksheet called 'Summary', column B needs to show the quantity of each inventory item that NewPlace holds in total across the three stores.

- Use 'copy' and 'paste link' on the data (do NOT use the Consolidate function) from the worksheets for each of the three stores, so that column B shows the total number of each item of inventory held.

- In column D of the same worksheet, use a formula to calculate the total cost of each inventory item and show the total cost of all inventory held. **(2 marks)**

(b)   In the Summary worksheet, freeze row 1 and 2 of the headings so that the headings remain visible when   scrolling down the list. To identify the high-value items of inventory, in cell C76 enter the formula that will   count the number of items where the cost of a single item of inventory exceeds £800.   **(1 mark)**

(c)   An analysis is required of the value of the inventory that NewPlace holds from non-furniture suppliers (NFS). For all the inventory items in the Summary worksheet EXCEPT any item supplied by DJ Furniture, insert a pivot chart and pivot table into a new worksheet. Produce a pivot chart of the total inventory cost for these suppliers.

- Rename this worksheet 'NFS Inventory'.

- Sort the row labels in the pivot table Z to A (Descending).

- Change the chart to a 3D exploded pie type.

- Add percentages to all the segments.

- Change York Retail segment only to bright yellow in colour.

- 3D rotate the pie so that York Retail segment is shown on the right hand side of the pie.

- Extract (explode) only the York Retail segment from the rest of the pie chart.

- Resize the pie chart so that all the segments can be clearly seen.

- Add the following title to the chart: 'Total inventory cost from non-furniture suppliers'.

- Move the chart legend to the bottom right hand corner.   **(4 marks)**

(d)   In the Summary worksheet, apply data validation for the whole of column E so that:

- Only the list of approved suppliers shown in cells G3:G7 can be used in a drop down box for each cell in column E.

- When you choose any cell in column E, the message 'Please choose from the drop down list' appears.

- A suitable warning is shown if users try to manually enter a supplier that is not on the approved list into any cell in column E.   **(2 marks)**

(e)   Ensure that only the list of approved suppliers in cells G3:G7 is protected using the password '123' so that nobody can change the list without this code.   **(1 mark)**

At the end of this task you should have one spreadsheet (saved as an .XLS or .XLSX file) to upload to the assessment environment. This should have five worksheets titled: 'NFS Inventory', 'Summary', 'Store 1', 'Store 2' and 'Store 3' with information and data in them.

TASK 2.2 (16 marks)

Download the spreadsheet file from the assessment environment. Save the spreadsheet file in the appropriate location, and rename it in the following format: 'your initial-surname-AAT no-dd.mm.yy-Task2.2'.

For example: J-Donnovan-123456-12.03.xx-Task2.2

A high degree of accuracy is required. You must save your work as an .XLS or .XLSX file at regular intervals to avoid losing your work.

You are Chris Makepeace, a part-qualified Accounting Technician. You work for NewPlace, a business which retails office equipment. NewPlace is owned and run by Mo Hussain.

You cover all aspects of bookkeeping and accounting for the business. NewPlace also uses the services of Addo & Co, a firm of accountants. Kiera Jackson is the accountant at Addo & Co who carries out tasks for NewPlace.

Today's date is 15 April 20X8.

Open your renamed spreadsheet file and choose the worksheet called 'Dec 20X8'. This contains data on the current budgeted performance of NewPlace for the six months ending 31 December 20X8. Mo Hussain has asked you to help revise some of the figures.

(a) Using the data available in the Dec 20X8 worksheet, complete the first pro forma to show Newplace's 'Current budgeted net profit/loss for the six months ended 31 December 20X8'. Show relevant cost sub- totals in column C as negative figures. **(2 marks)**

Mo has already increased the number of shop staff at the start of 20X8 and the cost of buying goods for resale has also gone up. To achieve a further increase in volume (and therefore profit) he is considering whether to increase store opening hours and improve the quality of customer service. To do this he needs to employ additional shop workers at an annual cost of £40,000 from 1 July 20X8.

In addition to the wages of the shop workers, these changes will have the following impact on the initial budgeted data set out at the top of the Dec 20X8 spreadsheet:

• increase average selling prices by 5%

• increase volume by 10%

• increase administration overheads by 4% (because of extra staff training).

(b) Assuming these changes take place, complete the second pro forma to show Newplace's 'Revised budgeted net profit/loss for six months ended 31 December 20X8'. Show relevant cost sub-totals in column C as negative figures. **(4 marks)**

(c) Apply conditional formatting to the revised budget you have produced in (b) to show any negative figures in red and bold font. **(2 marks)**

Mo is considering paying a bonus as an incentive to shop staff. If the increase in the revised budgeted sales in (b) is at least 15% more than the current budgeted sales figure in (a), Mo will consider paying a bonus of £0.05 per unit on all the units sold.

(d)   For the revised budget:

(i)   Use formulas to calculate the percentage change from the current budget (to two decimal places) for both:

- sales and

- net profit/loss.

Show the % change in cells B41 (sales) and B42 (net profit/loss) respectively.

(ii)   Use an IF statement in cell C41 to calculate any bonus payment due under the revised budget, showing EITHER the bonus amount payable if the percentage revenue change is greater than or equal to 15%, OR £0 if the percentage revenue change is less than 15%.   **(2 marks)**

(e)   Format all currency cells in the 'Dec 20X8' worksheet to GBP in the following format:

£##,### in whole numbers (no decimals). Ensure that the contents of every cell can be clearly seen. For the cells B27:C37 name this range 'Revised'.   **(2 marks)**

(f)   Use the pro forma contained in the worksheet called 'Email' to explain to Mo the financial effect of three of the proposed changes below on the business's current budgeted profit/loss for the six months ended 31 December 20X8. Choose any three changes from the following to explain in the email:

- sales volume

- sales price

- wages costs

- administration costs

- final profit/loss.   **(3 marks)**

(g)   Mo has found some terms that he does not fully understand and has asked you to explain these in the context of spreadsheets. Select the worksheet called Terminology. Choose one answer for each of the three questions. Ensure you answer 'Yes' to only one option for each question.   **(1 mark)**

At the end of this task you should have one spreadsheet (saved as an .XLS or .XLSX file) to upload to the assessment environment. This should have three worksheets titled: 'Dec 20X8', 'Email' and 'Knowledge', with information and data in them.

TASK 2.3 (14 marks)

Download the spreadsheet file from the assessment environment. Save the spreadsheet file in the appropriate location and rename it in the following format: 'your initial-surname-AAT no-dd.mm.yy-Task2.3'.

For example: J-Donnovan-123456-12.03.xx-Task2.3

A high degree of accuracy is required. You must save your work as an .XLS or .XLSX file at regular intervals to avoid losing your work.

For this task, you will also need to download the text file 'AVSY B2 Task 2.3 ETB 20x8.txt' from the assessment environment and save it in an appropriate location. You do not need to rename this file.

You are Chris Makepeace, a part-qualified Accounting Technician. You work for NewPlace, a business which retails office equipment. NewPlace is owned and run by Mo Hussain.

You cover all aspects of bookkeeping and accounting for the business. NewPlace also uses the services of Addo & Co, a firm of accountants. Kiera Jackson is the accountant at Addo & Co who carries out tasks for NewPlace.

Today's date is 15 January 20X9.

You are required to complete an extended trial balance for NewPlace for the year ended 31 December 20X8.

(a) Open your renamed spreadsheet file. Some of the information from the ledger accounts has already been populated in the extended trial balance worksheet named 'ETB'. However, some figures were placed in a text file, and as a result some of the ledger balances are missing.

- Select the second worksheet ('Sheet2').

- Rename this worksheet 'Subtotal'.

- Select cell D4 in the 'Subtotal' worksheet and import the downloaded text file called 'AVSY B2 Task 2.3 ETB 20x8.txt' from the appropriate location, starting in cell D4.

- Use 'copy' and 'paste link' to copy each of the amounts for purchases, wages and administration into the relevant cell in the ledger balances columns of the 'ETB' worksheet.

- In the 'Subtotal' worksheet, use the appropriate function to subtotal the Rent and Rates figures in the range D13:F21 for each change in 'Item'. Use the Sum function to add a subtotal to the cost column.

- Use 'copy' and 'paste link' to copy the Rent total and the Rates total into the appropriate cells in the ledger balances columns of the 'ETB' worksheet.

- In the 'ETB' worksheet, format all currency cells to Accounting style, in whole numbers (no decimals). Make sure that the contents of every cell can be clearly seen.

- Insert a formula in cell K5 that will always show the current date and time.

- In cell J32 insert a formula to show 'Balanced' if cell H32 and cell I32 are equal, and 'Error on ETB - Requires investigation' if not balanced. **(9 marks)**

(b)   This extended trial balance was constructed badly by a person who has since left the business.

- The correct figure for profit for the year has been calculated at £384,890. Insert this figure in the relevant cells of the 'ETB' worksheet.

- As well as the ledger balance omissions which you have corrected in part (a), there are also two errors in the last four columns of the extended trial balance, so the columns cannot balance.

  - Using relevant spreadsheet skills, together with your accounting knowledge, locate the errors. Correct them, so the contents of cell J32 will show 'Balanced' instead of 'Error on ETB - Requires investigation'.

  - Format the two cells which contain the corrected errors with a yellow fill background.

  - Custom format the contents of each corrected cell to show the font in magenta, keeping the Accounting style applied in (a).

- Explain the two errors that you found by writing your answer in the boxes shown in column K. Specifically state what accounting and spreadsheet skills you used to identify and correct them.   **(5 marks)**

At the end of this task you should have one spreadsheet (saved as an .XLS or .XLSX file) to upload to the assessment environment. This should have two worksheets titled 'ETB' and 'Subtotal', with information and data in them.

Section 8

SAMPLE ASSESSMENT 2 – ANSWERS

PART 1

TASK 1.1   (15 marks)

(a)   Complete the following statement   (2 marks)

To resolve the matter the conceptual framework states that Wajid must use…

his professional judgement.   ∇

(b)   Identify whether there is a conflict to be resolved   (2 marks)

Example of behaviour of Hook Ltd's management	Sherie's personal value	Is there a conflict to resolve?	
Long-standing employees are allowed an extra half day's holiday for every two years to permanent employment with Hook Ltd	Loyalty	No	∇
Employees are promoted on the basis of family or other close relationships	Fairness	Yes	∇

(c)   Identify whether the following statements are true or false   (3 marks)

Statement	True	False
Sherie may never disclose confidential information to any third party.		✓
The threat that Sherie is facing to her compliance with the fundamental principles is a self-interest threat.	✓	
Sherie must resign immediately from Hook Ltd as her integrity has been compromised by the offer from the potential customer.		✓

(d)   Complete the following statement   (2 marks)

Being offered gifts by the manager is | a familiarity threat ∇ | to Ian's fundamental

principle of | objectivity   ∇ |

(e) **Complete the following statement** (2 marks)

In relation to the evidence and documentation, Ian must be particularly careful to

ensure the fundamental principle of [confidentiality ∇] Is not breached

when seeking guidance from Antoine.

(f) **Complete the following statement** (2 marks)

Ellie has committed the criminal offence of [tipping off. ∇]

(g) **Complete the following statement** (2 marks)

Luke should disclose confidential information on this matter directly to

[the National Crime Agency. ∇]

TASK 1.2 (16 marks)

(a) **Show the entries that need to be made in the general ledger to correct the £2,000 VAT that was reclaimed.** (2 marks)

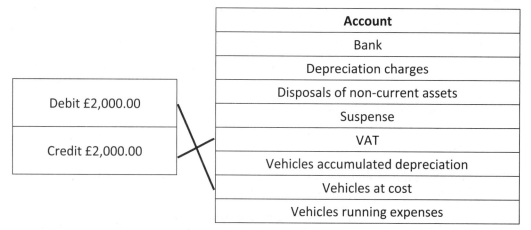

	Account
	Bank
	Depreciation charges
Debit £2,000.00	Disposals of non-current assets
	Suspense
	VAT
Credit £2,000.00	Vehicles accumulated depreciation
	Vehicles at cost
	Vehicles running expenses

(b) **Complete each of the following statements to show the action you advise.** (4 marks)

I advise that the VAT reclaim is an error that...

...can be ignored.	
...must be reported separately to HMRC.	✓
...can be corrected on the current VAT return without a separate report to HMRC.	

This action should be taken because...

...the error was deliberate.	✓
...of the size of the error.	
...Mo made a mistake that was reasonable in the circumstances.	

(c) According to the ethical code, which of your fundamental principles would be under threat if you called the helpline? **(1 mark)**

Objectivity	
Confidentiality	✓

(d) Do you need to take further action to ensure your compliance with the ethical code in this case? **(2 marks)**

No, no further action by me is necessary because it is Mo's responsibility to decide how to proceed.	
Yes, I should inform Mo in writing that my professional principles prevent me from being connected with the VAT return or other related information submitted to HMRC.	✓
Yes, I am obliged to inform HMRC about the error myself.	

(e) Answer to following:

(i) Prepare the journal for the first full year's depreciation on the car based on its corrected cost in the general ledger. **(4 marks)**

Journal

		Dr £	Cr £
Depreciation charges	∇	3,000	
Vehicles accumulated depreciation	∇		3,000

(ii) Complete the following statement about the overall effect on the business's profit for the year of correcting the VAT reclaim. **(1 mark)**

NewPlace's profit for the year will be [lower ∇] than if the VAT reclaim had not been corrected

(f) What should Kiera do next? **(2 marks)**

Discuss the matter in full with Mo.	
Make a Suspicious Activity Report to the relevant external authority, detailing her suspicions.	
Make an internal report within Addo & Co detailing her suspicions.	✓

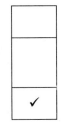

TASK 1.3 (15 marks)

(a) Using the information above, determine the following budgeted figures for the year to 31 December 20X7, to the nearest whole number. (4 marks)

(i)	Break-0even sales volume	12,000	units
(ii)	Total break-even contribution	£ 600,000	
(iii)	Total profit for the year	£ 400,000	
(iv)	Margin of safety	8,000	units

(b) Using the information from the trial balance, calculate the following actual figures for the year to 31 December 20X7. (4 marks)

(i)	Total variable cost	£	2,520,000
(ii)	Total fixed cost	£	438,000
(iii)	Total contribution	£	680,000
(iv)	Profit for the year	£	242,000

(c) To: Mo Hussain Mo.Hussaine@NewPlace.co.uk

From: Chris Makepeace Chris.Makepeace@NewPlace.co.uk

Date: 31.1.X8

Subject: Performance of NewPlace for 20X7

1	The budgeted profit for the year was £400,9000, whereas the actual profit achieved was only £242,000 (even though the budgeted volume of 20,000 units was achieved.

2	The revised break-even volume, using the actual figures, is 12,882 units. **Working** Actual contribution per unit = £680,000/20,000 units = £34 per unit Actual break-even sales volume = Fixed costs/Contribution per unit: £438,000/ £34 = 12,882 units.

3	The actual break-even volume of 12,882 units is higher than budgeted at 12,000 units and has been affected by the following changes compared to the budget: (i) Decreased fixed costs, which have fallen from £600,000 to £438,000, this reduces the break-even volume required. (ii) Much lower contribution per unit than budgeted, which increases the break-even volume required. Budgeted contribution per unit was £170 − £120 (or £600,000/12,000) or (£600,000 + £400,000)/20,000) = £50 per unit, compared to actual contribution of only £34 per unit. The reduced contribution per unit compared to the budget has been caused by a reduced average selling price per unit (budget £170, actual £3,200.000/20,000 = £160), plus an increased unit cost (budget £120, actual £2,520,000/20,000 = £16).

TASK 1.4   **(15 marks)**

(a)   **Threat 1**

> Janey's offer of expensive hospitality is a self-interest threat to my ethical principle of objectivity/integrity/professional behaviour. A self-interest threat occurs when a financial or other interest will inappropriately influence an accountant's judgement or behaviour. Janey called me several times to press for early payment, then she called me offering expensive hospitality. Clearly she was trying to influence my judgement with the offer.

Threat 2

> Janey's second call is an intimidation threat to my objectivity. An intimidation threat occurs when an accountant may be deterred from acting objectively by threats, whether actual or perceived. The original offer from her was not recorded so she could conceivably claim that I demanded the tickets. Saying that she would lie in this way to my employer was clearly an actual threat to intimidate me into making the payment.

Actions I should take

> I should use the Conceptual Framework to apply relevant safeguards to bring the threat to my principles down to an acceptable level OR I should use the ethical conflict resolution process stated in the code.
>
> I should follow any internal procedure for reporting/dealing with such threats.
>
> I should disclose what has happened to a colleague OR my line manager OR Mo OR AAT and seek advice as to what to do next.
>
> I should reject the offer of tickets.
>
> I should continue to arrange payments as DJ as normal.

(b)

To:	Mo Hussain Mo.Hussaine@NewPlace.co.uk
From:	Chris Makepeace Chris.Makepeace@NewPlace.co.uk
Date:	28/2/X8

Subject: | Accounting principles and financial information |

Thank you for your email of 28/2/X8

(1) | Two key assumptions:

Accrual/matching basis of accounting: we include transactions in the accounting period when they arise, not when they are paid in the form of cash.

For instance the 20X7 financial statements will include some items of inventory even though we have not yet paid the invoices from their suppliers.

Going concern assumption: we assume that the business will continue in operation for the foreseeable future, without the need to sell assets and pay liabilities at short notice.

If we did not assume this, the amounts we show for non-current assets, for example, would be different (market or 'fire sale' value rather than how much they cost when they were bought less depreciation).

(2) | EITHER

Relevance: financial information is relevant to the user if it is can make a difference to decisions made by the user. The information might be able to help them make decisions by predicting future o9utcomes (it has predictive value) or by confirming or changing their previous evaluations (it has confirmatory value).

OR

Faithful (re)presentation: the financial information is complete (it includes all necessary descriptions and explanations), neutral (without bias in how it is selected or presented) and free from error (no errors or omissions).

(3) | The statement of financial position (SFP) lists out your business's assets less its liabilities (including loans), so you can see how much the business is worth (its net asset value). It then shows how the net assets are funded – which is by your capital: the amounts you have introduced into the business plus the profits you have made and kept in the business.

(4) | The SFP links with the statement of profit or loss (SOPOL) via the profit figure. In the SOPOL the business's costs are deducted from its revenue to arrive at the profit for the period. In the SFP this figure is added to the capital you had in the business at the start of the period. Any amounts you have withdrawn in the period for your own use are deducted from this figure to arrive at your total capital.

OR

The SFP links with the statement of profit or loss (SOPOL) via the closing inventory figure. In the SOPOL the cost of closing inventory is deducted from the business's costs for 20X7. This is because its cost needs to be deducted from the revenue 20X8, when the inventory is actually sold. Instead the inventory is shown as an asset in the SFP for 20X7 to be carried forward and matched with revenue in 20X8.

Kind regards

Chris

PART 2

TASK 2.1

Row Labels	Sum of Total inventory Cost
York Retail	1401.69
Yellow Berry Ltd	3064.5
Recirc Ltd	10152.9
ABC Supplies	2298.28
Grand Total	**16917.37**

Assessor - Make sure DJ Furniture is not in the above list

Also ensure Row Labels are sorted Z to A

Sum of Total inventory Cost

Total inventory cost from non-furniture suppliers

Supplied by
- York Retail
- Yellow Berry Ltd
- Recirc Ltd
- ABC Supplies

8%

14%

18%

60%

Assessor - should be a 3D exploded pie chart

Chart title should be correct

York Retail segment should be yellow and on the right

York Retail segment must be separated from the rest of the chart

Legend should be in the bottom right corner

NFS Inventory / Summary / Store 1 / Store 2 / Store 3

Summary of Inventory

	Item description	Total number	Cost	Total inventory Cost	Supplied by		Approved Suppliers list
3	A4 ream bright white 80g	132	£1.80	£237.60	Yellow Berry Ltd		Yellow Berry Ltd
4	A4 ream bright white 100g	109	£1.90	£207.10	Yellow Berry Ltd		ABC Supplies
5	A3 ream bright white 80g	121	£2.20	£266.20	Yellow Berry Ltd		York Retail
6	A3 ream bright white100g	78	£2.60	£202.80	Yellow Berry Ltd		Recirc Ltd
7	A4 ream white 80g	75	£1.60	£120.00	Yellow Berry Ltd		DJ Furniture
8	A4 ream white 100g	149	£1.70	£253.30	Yellow Berry Ltd		
9	A3 ream white 80g	57	£2.10	£119.70	Yellow Berry Ltd		
10	A3 ream white 100g	85	£2.20	£187.00	Yellow Berry Ltd		
11	A4 ream yellow 80g	92	£2.20	£202.40	Yellow Berry Ltd		
12	A4 ream yellow 100g	56	£2.40	£134.40	Yellow Berry Ltd		
13	A3 ream yellow 80g	94	£2.50	£235.00	Yellow Berry Ltd		
14	A3 ream yellow 100g	119	£2.60	£309.40	Yellow Berry Ltd		
15	A4 ream blue 80g	97	£2.20	£213.40	Yellow Berry Ltd		
16	A4 ream blue 100g	88	£2.40	£211.20	Yellow Berry Ltd		
17	A3 ream blue 80g	66	£2.50	£165.00	Yellow Berry Ltd		
18	A3 ream blue 100g	80	£2.60	£208.00	ABC Supplies		
19	Binder 4 hole 50mm Black	79	£1.20	£94.80	ABC Supplies		
20	Binder 4 hole 50mm Red	138	£1.20	£165.60	ABC Supplies		
21	Binder 4 hole 50mm Green	39					
22	Binder 4 hole 75mm Black	63					
23	Binder 4 hole 75mm Red	45					
24	Binder 4 hole 75mm Green	71					
25	Pen Red pack of 5	105	£1.51	£158.55	York Retail		
26	Pen Black pack of 5	82	£1.51	£123.82	York Retail		
27	Pencil 2B pack of 10	101	£1.98	£199.98	York Retail		
28	Pencil H pack of 10	107	£1.98	£211.86	York Retail		
29	A4 ream blue card 250g	32	£2.90	£92.80	York Retail		
30	A4 ream yellow card 250g	27	£2.90	£78.30	York Retail		
31	Extor toner 2314	33	£12.50	£412.50	Recirc Ltd		
32	Extor toner 2598	34	£13.80	£469.20	Recirc Ltd		
33	Extor toner 3307a	17	£14.20	£241.40	Recirc Ltd		
34	Belay Cartridge Black 65a	28	£2.30	£64.40	Recirc Ltd		
35	Belay Cartridge Cyan 65a	22	£3.30	£72.60	Recirc Ltd		
36	Belay Cartridge Magenta 65a	25	£3.30	£82.50	Recirc Ltd		
37	Belay Cartridge Yellow 65a	21	£3.30	£69.30	Recirc Ltd		
38	Extor B/W printer 2300	3	£199.00	£597.00	Recirc Ltd		
39	Extor B/W printer 3658	4	£259.00	£1,036.00	Recirc Ltd		
40	Extor B/W printer 6280	4	£1,120.00	£4,480.00	Recirc Ltd		
41	Belay colour printer 65	3	£396.00	£1,188.00	Recirc Ltd		
42	Belay colour printer 105	3	£480.00	£1,440.00	Recirc Ltd		
43	Diary day to a page black	28	£0.56	£15.68	York Retail		
44	Diary day to a page red	40	£0.66	£26.40	York Retail		
45	Diary week to a page black	23	£1.80	£41.40	York Retail		

Assessor - check that rows 1 and 2 are frozen

Assessor - Check that ONLY these cells G3:G7 are protected by code 123 - you should be able to edit all others

Assessor - check that you can select any item in Column E and it will provide a drop down list

You should be prevented from entering anything other than the contents of the list

Assessor - try to insert "Dog" in this cell - you should get a suitable warning:-

Assessor - please check cell C76

Assessor
These cells should contain a formulas like –
= "Store 1"B10+"Store 2"B10+"Store 3"B10

Summary of Inventory

Item description	Total number	Cost	Total inventory Cost	Supplied by
Diary week to a page red	11	£1.80	£19.80	York Retail
Eraser pack of 5	31	£1.00	£31.00	York Retail
Scissors 15cm black	27	£5.65	£152.55	York Retail
Scissors 15cm black left hand	25	£6.85	£171.25	York Retail
Ruler steel 30cm	33	£1.89	£62.37	York Retail
Ruler non splinter 30cm	27	£0.59	£15.93	York Retail
Storage box 20x35x12 Red	21	£2.56	£53.76	ABC Supplies
Storage box 20x35x12 Black	35	£3.48	£121.80	ABC Supplies
Stapler size 41 Red	31	£6.21	£192.51	ABC Supplies
Stapler size 41 Blue	81	£6.21	£503.01	ABC Supplies
Paper clips 40mm (100)	38	£0.59	£22.42	ABC Supplies
Paper clips 25mm (100) mixed colours	123	£2.50	£307.50	ABC Supplies
Paper clips extra large (100)	31	£2.40	£74.40	ABC Supplies
Pencil sharpener Red	61	£0.59	£35.99	ABC Supplies
Pencil sharpener Black	41	£0.59	£24.19	ABC Supplies
Executive chair Black leather	33	£98.95	£3,265.35	DJ Furniture
Executive chair red back	9	£280.00	£2,520.00	DJ Furniture
3 drawer desk Glass top	32	£572.00	£18,304.00	DJ Furniture
4 drawer desk glass top	12	£350.00	£4,200.00	DJ Furniture
4 drawer filing cab lock black	21	£268.00	£5,628.00	DJ Furniture
2 drawer filing cab grey	60	£276.00	£16,560.00	DJ Furniture
10 draw filing cab grey	52	£899.00	£46,748.00	DJ Furniture
15 draw fining cab grey	36	£1,118.00	£40,248.00	DJ Furniture
Pedestal 3 draw black	32	£280.00	£8,960.00	DJ Furniture
Pedestal 2 draw black	24	£195.00	£4,680.00	DJ Furniture
Pedestal 3 draw oak effect	35	£350.00	£12,250.00	DJ Furniture
Main computer desk variable height Gl	16	£680.00	£10,880.00	DJ Furniture
6 door storage locker w/locks	14	£258.00	£3,612.00	DJ Furniture
6 door storage locker	9	£230.00	£2,070.00	DJ Furniture
Large double storage cupboard 3 shelve	5	£658.00	£3,290.00	DJ Furniture
		3	£200,132.72	

Approved Suppliers list

Assessor - check that rows 1 and 2 are frozen

Assessor – this cell should contain £200,132.72 with the formula = sum(D3:D75)

Assessor – This cell should contain the answer 3 and the formula =COUNTIF(C3:C75, >800")

Assessor - check one of the cells in column E, e.g. E79, to make sure the whole column has a drop down box

TASK 2.2

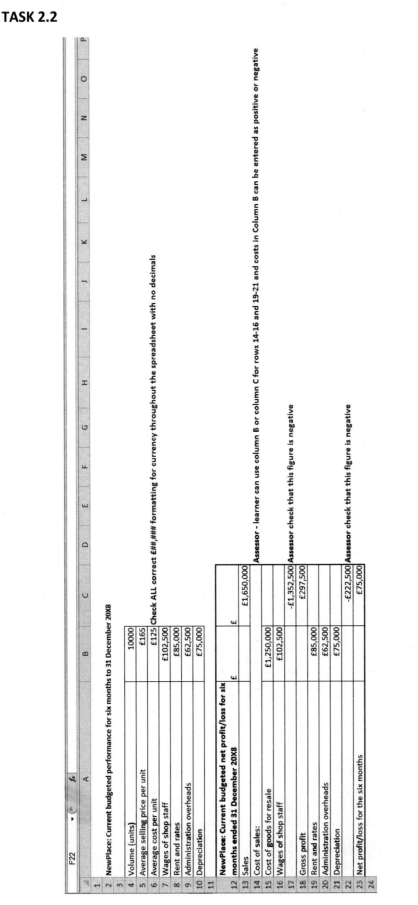

	A	B	C	D
	F22			
1				
2	NewPlace: Current budgeted performance for six months to 31 December 20X8			
3				
4	Volume (units)	10000		
5	Average selling price per unit	£165		
6	Average cost per unit	£125	Check ALL correct £##,### formatting for currency throughout the spreadsheet with no decimals	
7	Wages of shop staff	£102,500		
8	Rent and rates	£85,000		
9	Administration overheads	£62,500		
10	Depreciation	£75,000		
11				
12	NewPlace: Current budgeted net profit/loss for six months ended 31 December 20X8	£	£	
13	Sales		£1,650,000	
14	Cost of sales:			Assessor - learner can use column B or column C for rows 14-16 and 19-21 and costs in Column B can be entered as positive or negative
15	Cost of goods for resale	£1,250,000		
16	Wages of shop staff	£102,500		
17			-£1,352,500	Assessor check that this figure is negative
18	Gross profit		£297,500	
19	Rent and rates	£85,000		
20	Administration overheads	£62,500		
21	Depreciation	£75,000		
22			-£222,500	Assessor check that this figure is negative
23	Net profit/loss for the six months		£75,000	
24				

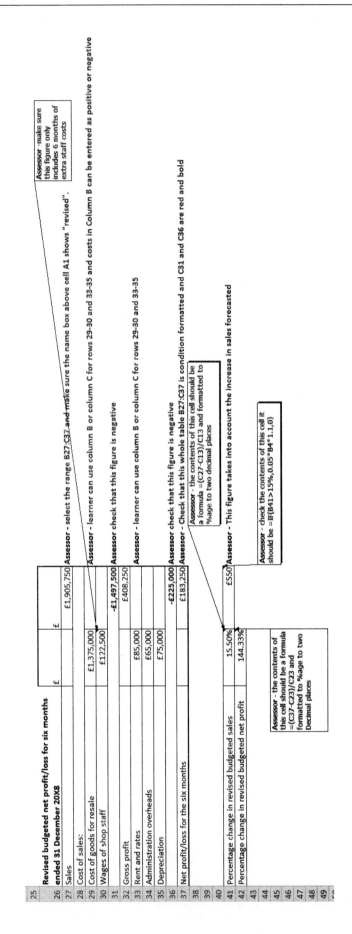

		£	£
25			
26	**Revised budgeted net profit/loss for six months ended 31 December 20X8**		
27	Sales		£1,905,750
28	Cost of sales:		
29	Cost of goods for resale	£1,375,000	
30	Wages of shop staff	£122,500	
31			-£1,497,500
32	Gross profit		£408,250
33	Rent and rates	£85,000	
34	Administration overheads	£65,000	
35	Depreciation	£75,000	
36			-£225,000
37	Net profit/loss for the six months		£183,250
38			
39			
40			
41	Percentage change in revised budgeted sales		15.50%
42	Percentage change in revised budgeted net profit		144.33%
43			
44			
45			
46			
47			
48			
49			

Assessor - make sure this figure only includes 6 months of extra staff costs

Assessor - select the range B27:C37 and make sure the name box above cell A1 shows "revised".

Assessor - learner can use column B or column C for rows 29-30 and 33-35 and costs in Column B can be entered as positive or negative

Assessor check that this figure is negative

Assessor - learner can use column B or column C for rows 29-30 and 33-35

Assessor check that this figure is negative

Assessor - Check that this whole table B27:C37 is condition formatted and C31 and C36 are red and bold

Assessor - the contents of this cell should be a formula =(C27-C13)/C13 and formatted to %age to two decimal places

Assessor - This figure takes into account the increase in sales forecasted

Assessor - check the contents of this cell it should be =IF(B41>15%,0.05*B4*1.1,0)

Assessor - the contents of this cell should be a formula =(C37-C23)/C23 and formatted to %age to two Decimal places

(f)

		Untitled - Message (HTML)
FILE	MESSAGE INSERT OPTIONS FORMAT TEXT REVIEW DEVELOPER Nuance PDF	

Clipboard — Basic Text — Names — Include — Tags — Zoom

From	Chris Makepeace <chris.makepeace@NewPlace.com>
To	Mo Hussain <Mo.Hussain@NewPlace.co.uk>
Subject	Report on estimated performance to December 20X8

Dear Mo, As requested I have explained the impact of three of the proposed changes:

Sales volume - will increase by 10% from 10,000 to 11,000 as we provide better customer service

Selling price - will increase from an average of £165 per unit to an average of £173.25 per unit (5%) as we provide better customer service

Wages of shop staff - will increase by £20,000 (19%) in the six months, from £102,500 to £122,500, as a result of staffing the extra opening hours

Admin costs - as a result of extra training to deliver better customer service, admin costs will rise £2,500 (4%) to £65,000.

Profit is now budgeted to rise by 144.33% from £75,000 to £183,250 as a result of the 15.5% increased sales (from £1,650,000 to £1,905,750) offset by the extra costs incurred to improved customer service.

(g)

Please indicate the correct answer in the box provided. You will get **no marks if you mark more than one box.**

Q1 What is a moving average?

Insert a YES in one box	**Description**
	A number that changes each time you enter data in a row
Yes	**A graph trendline showing accumulative changes in data**
	A formula that you can use in a column of data
	A number transferred to another worksheet

Q2 What is Rank and Percentile?

Insert a YES in one box	**Description**
	The ascending sorting of data in a column to show the top and bottom figures
	The relative sizes of segments in a pie chart
Yes	**The relative position of a value within a set of data**
	The sorting of data in a row

Q3 What is a Histogram?

Insert a YES in one box	**Description**
	A 3D exploded pie chart showing the relative sizes of data with percentages
	A link to another cell within a spreadsheet
	A set of old data shown in a spreadsheet
Yes	**A column chart of raw data that creates a picture of the data distribution**

TASK 2.3

NewPlace: Extended trial balance for the year 20X8

10/08/2016 10:43

Account name	Ledger balance Dr	Ledger balance Cr	Statement of profit or loss Dr	Statement of profit or loss Cr	Statement of Financial position Dr	Statement of Financial position Cr
Cash at bank	£ 12,780				£ 12,780	
Cash in hand	£ 3,450				£ 3,450	
Sales		£ 3,850,400		£ 3,850,400		
Capital		£ 364,810				£ 364,810
Purchases – goods for resale 1	£ 905,840		£ 905,840			
Purchases – goods for resale 2	£ 529,700		£ 529,700			
Purchases – goods for resale 3	£ 1,342,460	£ 2,780	£ 1,345,240			
Shop wages grade 1	£ 98,740		£ 98,740			
Shop wages grade 2	£ 137,760		£ 137,760			
Rent total	£ 140,000		£ 140,000			
Rates total	£ 32,000		£ 32,000			
Administration costs	£ 84,670	£ 1,450	£ 83,220			
Administration salaries	£ 45,210		£ 45,210			
Non-current assets	£ 920,000				£ 920,000	
Depreciation expense		£ 150,000	£ 150,000			
Accumulated depreciation	£ 450,000					£ 600,000
Purchase ledger control	£ 231,500					£ 231,500
Other payables – accruals		£ 2,780				£ 2,780
Sales ledger control	£ 415,600				£ 415,600	
Allowance for doubtful debts		£ 2,000		£ 2,000		
Irrecoverable debts expense		£ 2,000	£ 2,000			
Other receivables – prepaid		£ 1,450			£ 1,450	
Inventory	£ 178,500	£ 182,700	£ 178,500	£ 182,700	£ 182,700	
Drawings	£ 50,000				£ 50,000	
Profit		£ 384,890	£ 384,890			£ 384,890
	£ 4,896,710	£ 4,896,710	£ 338,930	£ 338,930	£ 4,033,100	£ 4,033,100	£ 1,585,980	£ 1,585,980	Balanced

Assessor to check format of currency with zero decimals, and all contents seen (a)

Assessor to check that F31 and I31 have the correct amount entered (b)

Assessor
This cell should contain the formula =NOW()

Assessor
At least one explanation must show that the learner has used either trace precedents or show formulas or formula auditing

Assessor
Check that cells B11:B15 are linked to Subtotal worksheet – e.g. =SubtotalE4

Assessor
Check that cells B11:B19 are linked to Subtotal worksheet – e.g. =SubtotalE4

Assessor this cell should contain the format [Magenta] £ " #,##0 – not just used coloured font. Fill must be yellow

Assessor this cell should contain the format [Magenta] £ " #,##0 not just used coloured font. Fill must be yellow

Assessor
This cell should = £ 1,585,980

Assessor – this cell should contain a full IF statement =IF(H32=I32,"Balanced","Error on ETB – requires investigation")

Explanation for error 1 – admin costs. Key words are in red

I used trace precedents and show formulas to find that the formula for Admin costs in cell F18 in the Statement of profit or loss showed the credit adjustment of £1450 being added to the debit ledger balance instead of being subtracted from it. Since the £1450 adjustment is a credit, it should be deducted from the ledger balance.

Explanation for error 2: accrual Key words are in red

Other payables – accruals in H24 was shown as a debit balance in the Statement of financial position whereas it should be in the credit column, in I24. It is possible to find this error using accounting knowledge (accruals are credit balances in the SOFP) or using show formulas to identify that the original reference in column H (a debit) was to column E (a credit).

H ◄ ► ►I ETB | ETB | Subtotal

M39

	A	B	C	D	E	F	G	H	I	J	K
1											
2											
3											
4				Purchases - goods for resale 1	905840						
5				Purchases - goods for resale 2	529700						
6				Purchases - goods for resale 3	1342460						
7				Shop wages grade 1	98740						
8				Shop wages grade 2	137760						
9				Administration costs	84670						
10				Administration salaries	45210						
11											
12											
13				Item	Shop	Cost					
14				Rent	Shop 1	21000					
15				Rent	Shop 2	25600					
16				Rent	Shop 3	35200					
17				Rent	Shop 4	58200					
18				**Rent Total**		140000					
19				Rates	Shop 1	4800					
20				Rates	Shop 2	5850					
21				Rates	Shop 3	8050					
22				Rates	Shop 4	13300					
23				**Rates Total**		32000					
24				**Grand Total**		172000					
25											
26											

Assessor –
check that this cell contains the formula
=SUBTOTAL(9,F14:F17)